TOLSTOY IN LONDON

Tolstoy in London

VICTOR LUCAS

Evans Brothers Limited London

Published by Evans Brothers Limited
Montague House, Russell Square,
London, WC1B 5BX

Set in 12 point Apollo by Filmtype Services
Limited, Scarborough and printed in Great
Britain by T. & A. Constable Limited
Hopetoun Street, Edinburgh EH7 4NF

Lucas, Victor
Tolstoy in London.
1. Tolstoy, Leo, *Count* — Homes and haunts —
England — London
I. Title
891.7'3'3   PG3401

ISBN 0–237–44979–X   PRA 6596

Contents

Acknowledgements

The author would like to acknowledge the help of Iona and Peter Opie, Mary Melvin and Miss Pollard of Trinity College Library, Dublin, and Miss Constance M. Hayward of The Chelsea Society.

For permission to reproduce copyright illustrations the author and publishers gratefully acknowledge the following:

Battersea District Library; page 85
The British Library; page 34 **(bottom)**
The Guildhall Library, City of London; page 25, 29
Hammersmith Library; page 86
The Illustrated London News; page 26, 47, 48
Kensington and Chelsea Libraries; page 8, 52, 59, 65, 71, 73
The Mansell Collection; page 30 **(bottom)**
Mary Evans Picture Library; page 30 **(top)**, 87
Novosti Press Agency; page 10, 12 **(left)**, 95, 107, 108
Punch; page 51
Radio Times Hulton Picture Library; page 32, 39, 40, 41, 45, 46, 84
Royal Holloway College, University of London; page 23
Society for Cultural Relations with the U.S.S.R.; page 11, 12 **(right)**, 13, 15, 18, 97, 100, 106
The Times; page 21, 22, 34 **(top)**
Trinity College, Dublin; page 80, 81

For quotations in this book the author and publishers gratefully acknowledge the following:

John Calder Ltd for **Summer Impressions** by Fyodor Dostoevsky, translated by Kyril FitzLyon
Doubleday and Company Inc. and W. H. Allen Ltd for **Tolstoy** by Henri Troyat, translated by Nancy Amphoux. Copyright © 1967 by Doubleday and Company Inc.
Hutchinson Publishing Group Ltd for **Married to Tolstoy** by Lady Cynthia Asquith
New American Library, Inc., for **Fables and Fairy Tales** by Leo Tolstoy and translated by Ann Dunnigan. Copyright © 1962 by Ann Dunnigan
Oxford University Press for **The Life of Tolstoy** by Aylmer Maude
Penguin Books Ltd for **Childhood, Boyhood, Youth** by L. N. Tolstoy translated by Rosemary Edmonds © 1964 by Rosemary Edmonds, and for **Anna Karenin** by L. N. Tolstoy translated by Rosemary Edmonds, © 1954, 1978 by Rosemary Edmonds

Introduction

In the Spring of 1861 a Russian aristocrat spent sixteen days in London. He was thirty-two years of age, he spoke and read English, and he was passionately interested in education. He wasn't yet known outside Russia as a writer. His early works had not yet been translated into English, and it was not until two years later that he began *War and Peace*. At his request, Matthew Arnold, the poet, who was then a senior official of the Department of Education, gave him a letter of introduction to a number of schools for the children of the artisan and tradesman class. Arnold referred to him in the letter simply as 'A Russian gentleman, Count Leon Tolstoy . . .'

We tend to think of Tolstoy as an aged greybeard with bags under his eyes, as seen in photographs and the earliest newsreels. But that is only the mask which Nature puts on people when they grow old. The reality is hidden underneath. To find that reality we have to look at him as his contemporaries saw him, and as his wife and children saw him.

He was other things besides a writer. In his youth he was a soldier and fought in the Crimea. He served for a time in the notorious Fourth Bastion, known to the British as Flagstaff Bastion, a strong point and death trap on the hills overlooking Sevastopol. There he worked on a delicate and moving account of his own boyhood, while the British and French artillery lobbed grenades over the parapet. It was during his time in the Crimea that he wrote also his *Sevastopol Sketches*, a devastating exposure of the stupidity and wastefulness of war. He was soon to condemn all forms of violence, yet he was himself, throughout his long life, a man of the most violent promptings. He was, in addition, a romantic.

When this complex genius arrived in London in 1861 he was a striking, still young and not unhandsome man, with a black beard and piercing eyes. Among the schools he visited was the Practising School attached to the College of St. Mark in Chelsea. The building is still there today, a fascinating octagonal structure, its design inspired by that of the Baptistry in Florence. Its unusual features included eight curtained alcoves, one for each class, radiating from the

The octagonal building of St. Mark's Practising School

eight-sided central stove containing a bake-oven in which the children could keep their pies warm until lunch time.

On 12 March 1861 Tolstoy spoke with the boys of Class 3B. He asked them each to write him an essay on what they had done that day, and on things of interest they had seen on their way to school; an essay we have all written in our time. Those they wrote for the Russian gentleman are very short, and some come to an abrupt end, almost as soon as they have begun, interrupted by the bell.

They were written on small sheets of cheap classroom paper, in the standard copper-plate handwriting of schoolchildren of those days. Some of them wrote criss-cross to save paper, the custom of an earlier period before the introduction of the penny post. It is interesting to find some of the boys, as late as 1861, following what was presumably the lifelong habit of their parents.

Tolstoy took these small scraps of paper back to Russia with him, back to his estate at Yasnaya Polyana. Incredibly, no one in England appears to have been aware of their existence, or of the Tolstoy connection with the school. They were, it seems, quite unknown to all those many writers who have over the years produced biographies of Tolstoy. The school itself, no longer occupying the original building, brought out in 1973 an interesting and detailed account of its history, which contains no mention of the Russian's visit that day in March 1861.

I only learned of the essays myself in 1976, when I was lecturing on Tolstoy for the British Library, as an accompaniment to the Library's Tolstoy Exhibition in the Special Exhibitions Gallery of the British Museum. Most of the exhibits were loaned by the Tolstoy Museums in the U.S.S.R. and among the many items on display were these faded essays, written a hundred and fifteen years earlier. They had returned to England for the first time, and are now back in Russia.

———◇◇◇◇◇———

How do you educate a child? Do you say to that child, 'This is what you will learn, not other things, however much they may interest you, but this which we adults say will equip you for life and enable you to prosper in the system which we have created and into which you have been born. If you study diligently and ask only the questions you are required to ask, and do not waste our time by asking other more awkward ones, and if you cultivate a retentive memory for facts and figures, then you will succeed in passing severe tests known as examinations, and you will set foot on the ladder leading upwards. If, instead, you do not do these things, then you will descend the ladder leading downwards.'

Tolstoy would have none of this. He believed that you should encourage a child to ask questions about every aspect of life. You encourage the child's curiosity, its creative imagination, and you try your best to answer his or her questions honestly and truthfully. Even if the questions are 'Why should I ask questions?' 'Why should I come to school?' 'Why shouldn't I play truant instead?' 'Why should I believe a word you say?' And in the process, if you are a good teacher, not only do you educate the child but that child educates you.

To say that his educational methods were a hundred years ahead of their time would be to imply that we are ready for them now, and alas we are not. Neither

Tolstoy

in capitalist nor in communist countries can we afford to allow children to learn what they wish to learn. We insist that they must prepare for a useful function in society. Upon our terms, and judged by our adult criteria of what is most desirable. No bad thing, perhaps, wisely and imaginatively applied. As we know to our cost, in our own time, to depart from it can lead to anarchy in the classroom. But Tolstoy had a vision of something better. It may be at present unattainable but that vision should not be lost sight of.

—◦◦◇◦◦—

His Early Life

e was born an aristocrat in 1828, and he became by inheritance a landowner. The owner, too, of large numbers of serfs on the family estates at Yasnaya Polyana, about 130 miles south of Moscow. His father, Count Nikolai Tolstoy, who had served in the 1812 war against Napoleon, died when his son was only nine. His mother had died when he was an infant, too young to retain any memory of her. She was a Volkonski, a member of a noble family which had had great influence at the court of Catherine the Great, and which traced its ancestry back to Rurik the Viking, who had come to Russia a thousand years before. An orphan, the young Tolstoy was brought up by an aunt. He attended the University of Kazan, where the subjects he studied included Oriental languages. He was unhappily conscious at this time of what he considered to be his own ugliness, and his inferiority in every way to his three older brothers.

The Tolstoy brothers, (*l–r*) Sergei, Nikolai, Dmitry, and Leo

A page from the manuscript of *Youth*.

Tolstoy in 1853.

His first attempt to teach the children on his estates was made as early as 1848, when he was a young man of twenty. Finding himself inadequate to the task, and aware of his lack of qualifications, he closed the school, a converted bedroom in the house, and followed his brother Nikolai into the army.

He served first in the Caucasus, that spectacular and wildly beautiful region in the mountains between the Black Sea and the Caspian, north of Persia. It exerted the same almost magical hold over those Russians who served there as the North West Frontier of India, not all that far away, did over the British. As a cadet serving with a battery of light mountain guns he was to have experiences in the Caucasus which he would find of value when he came to write *The Cossacks* and *Hadji Murad*.

He lived the usual life of a young Russian army officer in his early twenties; spells of action against the mountain tribes, bouts of heavy drinking, and he acquired a hearty appetite for the free and independent Cossack girls of the villages. Which brings us to the fact that he began writing in an army clinic, where he was recovering from the fearsome treatment used in those days as the cure for venereal disease. He put his enforced idleness to good use, writing there in the clinic *Childhood*, the first part of his largely autobiographical trilogy, *Childhood, Boyhood, Youth*, a delightful book of much sensitivity and a

The Fourth Bastion at Sevastopol

great deal of gentle humour. It is perhaps significant that at such an early age, and under such unfortunate circumstances, he should have chosen as his subject this delicate and moving account of a young child growing towards adolescence.

Then came the Crimean War, and while Cardigan and Raglan were muddling their way towards Sevastopol this young Russian officer was gaining there first-hand experience of a full-scale war, which he would draw upon when he came to write *War and Peace* and recreate the battles of Schöngraben, Austerlitz, and Borodino. In the Fourth Bastion, among scenes of carnage and death, he wrote much of *Boyhood*, the second part of his trilogy. It was here too that he wrote the work that was to make him famous, his *Sevastopol Sketches*. These were published in instalments in St. Petersburg and Moscow, and they created a sensation; nothing like them had ever been written before. For the first time, civilians safe at home, far from the fighting, were able to learn what it was really like to be in the line, facing the enemy guns.

> You will see war, not as a splendid array of troops in beautiful formation, with music and the beating of drums, fluttering colours and generals on prancing steeds, but war in its true aspect — blood, suffering, and death . . .[1]

This was no pretty fiction about honour and glory and the delights of dying for the Tsar. It was reporting of a very high order, written by a young man with an uncompromising directness, and yet with an awareness of the vulnerability of human beings. He had become a self-appointed war correspondent, praising the courage of the Russian peasant in his conscript's uniform, but concealing nothing of the brutality and the stupidity of war. He referred to himself as 'cannon fodder of the most useless kind'[2], but he went on writing it all down while the grenades exploded and the cannon balls fell among the gun emplacements.

More thoughts were already stirring in the mind of this unusual young man. He writes in his diary:

> A stupendous idea to the realisation of which I feel capable of devoting my life. That idea is the founding of a new religion . . . the religion of Christ but purged of dogmas and mysticism, – a practical religion, not promising future bliss but giving bliss on earth . . . *Deliberately* to contribute to the union of man by religion is the basic thought which I hope will dominate me.[3]

He was just twenty-six, and his life was already being dominated by a passion for gambling. Dostoevsky was not the only great Russian writer to be bitten by that particular bug. He was heavily involved at the card tables in Sevastopol on a scale which even his fellow officers found staggering. To pay his gambling debts he borrowed a large sum of money, pledging as security the family home at Yasnaya Polyana, where he had been born, and which he had inherited from his father. With the money he obtained he did not, after all, settle his debts. Instead, he gambled again – and lost it all. The new owner dismantled much of the house, which was built of wood, and took it away to re-erect it on another site, leaving behind the much smaller two-storied building which was to be Tolstoy's home for the rest of his life. From that time, whenever we hear of the house at Yasnaya Polyana it is this smaller building; the main house, built by his grandfather, was lost to the Tolstoys for ever. Not long afterwards, he wrote an account of what it is to be a compulsive gambler, in his story *Notes of a billiard marker*. You get just a hint of it also in *War and Peace*, in the scene in which young Nicolai Rostov, to his horror, loses 43,000 roubles at cards.

A fellow officer who served with him in the Fourth Bastion recorded his impressions of Tolstoy at this time.

> After a few days' leave he would return to the mess and taking me aside, quite apart, begin his confessions. He would tell me all: how he had caroused and gambled, and where he had spent his days and nights; and all the time, if you will believe me, he would condemn himself, and suffer as though he

Contributors to *Sovremennik* (Contemporary) magazine founded by Pushkin.
Seated (*l–r*): I. Goncharov, I. Turgenev, A. Druzhin, A. Ostrovsky
Standing: L. Tolstoy, D. Grigorovich

were a real criminal. He was so distressed that it was pitiful to see him. That's
the sort of man he was. In a word, a queer fellow, and to tell the truth one I
could not quite understand. He was, however, a rare comrade, a most
honourable fellow, and a man one can never forget.[4]

He was in Sevastopol on the day it fell to the advancing British and French
troops. This was the end of the war. The Tsar sued for peace, and Tolstoy, the
young artillery officer, the man of the hour, went to St. Petersburg, there to be
welcomed and fêted in all the drawing-rooms as a literary lion. He mixed with
the established writers of the time, among whom was Turgenev, who said of
him, 'When this young wine ripens it will be a drink fit for the Gods!'[5] They
found him, however, uncompromisingly dogmatic, aggressively dynamic; they
could sense in him the earthquake, the tidal wave, he was to become.

15

In Petersburg he did everything to excess, as usual. Drinking prodigiously, gambling, quarrelling, and spending much of his time in both high class and low class brothels. He was at a loss, the war was over and he thought he had written himself out. He resigned his commission and went to Paris for a time, indulging there in very much the same activities as in Petersburg. A few weeks in Switzerland and then he returned to his estates at Yasnaya Polyana. There he began an involvement with a young peasant woman, the wife of one of his serfs. He had a son by her, who grew up to be a coachman on the estate. Her name was Aksinya, and it is possible that she may have meant more to him than any other woman in his life. Certainly his feelings for her went very deep and were more than physical. I am in love as never before, he wrote in his diary. Years later his wife was to be intensely jealous of the relationship, even though it had ended with his marriage.

Over the next year or so he wrote several stories, and the exquisite short novel *Family Happiness*, which he wrote in the first person singular as a young girl; writing with an affectionate insight into her emotions which is at once moving and remarkable. But then this egocentric man always had the ability to step outside of himself into the very soul of another person, the mind of another creature, whether it be the retired judge Ivan Ilyich, or Vronsky's thorough-bred racehorse in *Anna Karenina*.

Distant, domineering, though he often was, concealing his vulnerability beneath a surface arrogance, there was also an unexpected warmth in him. It came through in his relations with the Cossack troops under his command and with some, at any rate, of his many women, and above all with children. He always got on very well with children. With them he could relax.

On his return from the war in the Crimea, he had found the village children were still being taught by semi-illiterates, or at best by uneducated retired soldiers and minor church functionaries. Sometimes the education consisted solely of giving the children prayers to learn by heart. If they were unable to commit them to memory they were beaten or made to kneel in the corner on hard dried peas.

He re-opened his own school at Yasnaya Polyana, and painstakingly devoted himself to reading everything he could find about methods of education.

> Without any preconceived theories or views on the subject I . . . was confronted with two questions: (1) What must I teach? and (2) How must I

teach it? In the whole mass of people who are interested in education there exists ... the greatest diversity of opinions ... Every educationist of every given school firmly believed that the methods he used were the best, because they were founded on absolute truth ... [When] I became a schoolmaster in a village popular school in the backwoods ... I was aided by a certain tact in teaching with which I am gifted, and especially by that close and passionate interest which I took in the subject.

        • • •

When I entered at once into the close and direct relations with those forty tiny peasants that formed my school (I called them tiny peasants because I found in them the same characteristics of perspicacity, the same immense store of information from practical life, of jocularity, simplicity, and loathing for everything false, which distinguishes the Russian peasant) when I saw their susceptibility, their readiness to acquire the information which they needed, I felt at once that the antiquated church method of instruction had outlived its usefulness to them .... Because compulsion in education ... is repulsive to me, I did not exercise any pressure, and the moment I noticed that something was not readily received, I did not put any compulsion on the pupils, but looked for something else.

It appeared to me ... that nearly everything which in the educational world was written about schools was separated by an immeasurable abyss from the truth .... I found no sympathy in all the educational literature ... but simply complete indifference, in regard to the question which I put .... I was young then and this indifference grieved me. I did not understand that when I asked them 'How do you know what to teach and how to teach?' I was like a man who, let us say, in a gathering of Turkish pashas, who were discussing the question in what manner they could collect the greatest amount of revenue from the people, should make them the following proposition: 'Gentlemen, before considering how much revenue to collect from each, we must first analyse the question on what your right to exact that revenue is based.' Obviously all the pashas would continue their discussion of the measures of extortion, and would reply only with silence to his irrelevant remark.[6]

⸺◦⬦◦⸺

In July 1860, after two years practical experience of teaching, he left Russia in order to learn all that personal observation could tell him about education in other countries. First he went to Germany, where he was appalled by the strictness in the classrooms. He writes in his travelling notes:

I visited a school [in Saxony]. It was dreadful. Prayers for the King, whippings, everything learnt by heart, frightened, mentally distorted children. Coercion is used in schools when there is no respect for the human nature of the children.[7]

In Kissingen he met Julius Froebel, the German sociologist, nephew of Friederich Froebel who had founded the Kindergarten. He surprised Froebel by his unorthodox views. In Germany, as elsewhere, professional teachers looked at him askance. He told Froebel:

> Education ... will give better results in our country than in Germany, because Russian people are not yet perverted ... Popular instruction must not be compulsory. If it is any good then the need of it must be born of itself, just as the desire of nutrition is created by hunger.[8]

In September 1860 he was at Hyères in the South of France, and it was here that there occurred an event which was to mark him for life; the death in his arms of his brother Nikolai of tuberculosis. A composite of that death and the death of another brother, Dmitri, figures in *Anna Karenina* as the death of Levin's brother Nikolai, and it is, in my opinion, the most truthful, the most unsentimental and the most moving account of a death ever written. There are a great many chapters in that book; only one of them was given a title by its author, and that title is 'Death'.

Tolstoy, left, with his brother Nikolai in 1851

There followed a time of indecision, of depression. 'I try to write, I force myself, and I can't do it . . . Nikolai's death has hit me harder than anything I have ever experienced . . .'[9] He stayed on at Hyères for a time, surrounded by consumptives, seemingly unable to leave. He went for long walks, spending much of his time with the nine year old son of an acquaintance. They went together to Porquerolles, and to the castle of the Trou des Fées. The boy was at Hyères because of a lung complaint. Sometimes Tolstoy would carry him on his shoulders, telling him on the way stories of a magic golden horse and of a great oak tree from the top of which one could see all the cities of the world, all its oceans and plains and mountains. Shortly before the year's end he left Hyères to resume his detailed investigation of the effectiveness or otherwise of the educational systems of Europe.

—◇◇◇◇—

He describes his impressions of Marseilles:

> I visited all the schools for the working people of that city. . . . The school programme consists in learning by heart the catechism, biblical and universal history, the four operations of arithmetic, French orthography, and book-keeping. . . . To questions from the history of France they answered well by rote, but if I asked anything at haphazard, I received such answers as that Henry IV. had been killed by Julius Caesar. . . .

> In Marseilles I also visited a lay school and also a monastic school for grown persons. . . . The instruction is the same: mechanical reading . . . book-keeping . . . religious instruction and so forth. After the lay school I saw the daily instruction offered in the churches; I saw the *salles d'asile*, in which four-year-old children, at a given whistle, like soldiers, made evolutions around the benches, at a given command lifted and folded their hands, and with strange quivering voices sang laudatory hymns to God and to their benefactors, and I convinced myself that the educational institutions of the city of Marseilles were exceedingly bad.

> If, by some miracle, a person should visit all these establishments, without having seen the people in the streets, in their shops, in the cafés, in their home surroundings, what opinion would he form of a nation which was educated in such a manner? He certainly would conclude that that nation was ignorant, rude, hypocritical, full of prejudices, and almost barbarous. But it is enough to enter into relations with and talk to a common man, to be convinced that the French nation is, on the contrary, almost such as it regards itself to be: intelligent, clever, affable, free from prejudices, and really civilised. Look at a city workman of about thirty years of age: he will

write a letter without such mistakes as are made at school, often without any mistakes at all; he has an idea of politics, consequently of modern history and geography; he knows more or less history from novels; he has some knowledge of the natural sciences. He frequently draws and applies mathematical formulae to his trade. Where did he learn all this?

I found an answer to it in Marseilles without trouble when, after the schools, I began to stroll down the streets, to frequent the dram-shops, *cafés chantants*, museums, workshops, quays and bookstalls. The very boy who told me that Henry IV. had been killed by Julius Caesar knew very well the story of *The Three Musketeers* and of *Monte Cristo*. I found twenty-eight illustrated editions of these in Marseilles, costing from five to ten centimes. . . . In addition there are . . . the public libraries and the theatres. Then the cafés . . . in each of these cafés they give little comedies and scenes and recite verses. Taking the lowest calculation, we get one-fifth of the population who get their daily oral instruction, just as the Greeks and Romans were instructed, in their amphitheatres.

Whether this education is good or bad is another matter; but here it is, this unconscious education, which is so much more powerful than the one by compulsion.[10]

He concluded that people learn of their own volition, and that the novel is a powerful factor in education, simply because it shapes people's minds.

Next he went to Italy; to Florence, Naples, and Rome. Years later he was to tell of how he was standing on the summit of the hill of the Pincio, with the city of Rome spread before him in all its ancient splendour, when he suddenly heard a small child weeping. As an old man he was unable to remember the classical ruins which had so impressed him, the temples, the obelisks and fountains, but could recall only the dirty, tear-stained face of the child, with all the sorrows of the human race in its crying.

On to Paris in February, a city he knew well, and there he visited more schools. London was his next port of call. He arrived in agony with the toothache from which he suffered throughout much of his life.

—◇◇◇—

Nineteenth-Century England

The England in which Tolstoy spent his sixteen days in Spring 1861 was very much on the move, gathering that momentum which would culminate thirty-six years later in all the pride and bombast of Queen Victoria's Diamond Jubilee.

Not that everyone was getting rich, or even staying rich, on the great Victorian bandwagon of material achievement. Every few years throughout the sixties, as had been the case in the forties and fifties, the newspapers tell of commercial panic, of the bankrupting of investors (especially those in railway stock), of widespread unemployment, and in some cases of actual starvation among the poor. For many, however, the Victorian heyday seemed well under way again after the temporary checks to its *amour-propre* occasioned by the shocking events at Meerut and Cawnpore and Miss Nightingale's revelations of bungling at Scutari.

Like any other visitor to a foreign capital, who has some knowledge of the language, Tolstoy would presumably have bought himself a newspaper upon arrival, almost certainly *The Times*, to find out what was going on, what the locals were discussing. In those days the actual news was inside the paper. The front page of *The Times* contained not headlines but boxed announcements, advertisements and items of a more personal nature.

There were various ways in which the enterprising could make a living, from finding dogs before they were lost to arousing the curiosity of the gullible.

STRAYED, on the 27th February, from No. 10, Rutland-mews south, Knightsbridge, a large BLACK NEWFOUNDLAND DOG, with collar engraved " Duke, Oswald Augustus Smith, Blendon-hall, Kent." Whoever brings the dog to 10, Rutland-mows south, will be REWARDED.

CAME ASTRAY, a handsome and valuable DOG, of a rare breed. The owner can have it by giving a description and paying all expenses. Apply at the Waggon and Horses, Kewbridge, Brentford.

THE NEW DISCOVERY.—LINDORFF's ingenious and wonderful INVENTION for TAKING PORTRAITS and LANDSCAPES by day or night, without apparatus. The whole secret, with instructions and specimens, forwarded for 25 stamps.— H. W. Lindorff, drawing academy, 2, Dennark-hill, Camberwell.

TEN SHILLINGS REWARD.——LOST, TWO BANK POST BILLS, No. M. 555, dated 20th Feb., 1860, £10, and No. M. 564, of the same date, £15. Whoever will bring them to the office of Messrs. Maude and Hallett, Great George-street, Westminster, shall receive the above reward. Payment has been stopped.

CIRCULARS.—To H. A. M. and M. H. M., who LEFT HOME on Friday afternoon.—If you ever wish to see your mothers again alive, you must RETURN at once. They are both very ill, and the doctor says it is impossible for them to live (perhaps not many hours), unless you come home at once. If you have no means to return get some kind friend to telegraph to us, and they shall be rewarded for their trouble. All will be forgiven.

FIVE POUNDS REWARD.--MISSING, a YOUNG MAN and GIRL. The former is about 5ft. 11in. high, 19 years of age, dressed in black frock coat, dark waistcoat and trousers, and Scotch cap; hair cut short, has a scar on his left cheek. The female about 5ft. high, 16 years of age, dressed in mourning, with sealskin cloak, trimmed with violet-coloured silk on the sleeves; fair and pale looking. The above reward will be paid to any one who will give any information that will lead to their recovery to H. Whale, 56, Regent-street, W.

FIVE HUNDRED POUNDS REWARD.—— TEAGUE, CHARLES BROOKS, late of Crown-court, Cheapside, in the city of London, solicitor, deceased.—The above sum will be paid to any person giving such information as will lead to the absolute discovery of who were the TRUSTEES of a DEED of SETTLEMENT of a large sum in Consols, made by the above-named gentleman some few years since for the benefit of his wife and children; also, as one of the trustees died in 1857, what was his name, address, and date of his death, or the name and address of the present surviving trustee, on application to Messrs. Nethersole and Owen, of No. 1, New-inn, Strand, solicitors to the widow and executrix of the late Charles Brooks Teague.

TO M. E. B.—Consider the rash step you have taken! You cannot be predestined for this. Use your free will, and RETURN at once. Rely on my promise. You shall be affectionately received, and all forgiven. At least communicate immediately with your friends, and relieve their anxiety.—N. B.

For a combination of mystery, chicanery, and marital intrigue the front page of *The Times* could hardly be bettered. One can see where Dickens got his plots from.

It is very likely that he also bought a copy of the highly regarded weekly, *The Illustrated London News*. This appeared only on Saturdays and was much esteemed, not only for the quality of its reporting, but for the many graphic drawings by a team of first-class illustrators. Unlike *The Times*, it put its main stories squarely on the front page.

The Illustrated London News, 2 March 1861

Emancipation of Serfs in Russia

Tomorrow morning nearly forty millions of the human family who tonight will retire to bed as slaves will rise up free. The 3rd. of March (Feb. 19th Old Style) has been fixed upon for the emancipation of serfs throughout the Russian Empire.

A week later there was a large item relating to the arts:

All the world – by which we mean the artistic profession and the picture-seeing public generally – is on the *qui vive* about Mr. Frith's promised great work entitled 'Life at a Railway Station', for which ... he has received a commission from Mr. Flatow, at the unprecedented price of eight thousand seven hundred and fifty guineas.

We are satisfied that with pictures, as with other commodities, the value is 'just as much as they will bring'; and we have no doubt that Mr. Flatow, with his sound practical knowledge, has made a pretty safe calculation of his chances of gain or loss in the transaction. The return anticipated to be made out of the picture will be derived first from the exhibition of the picture in London and the Provinces, secondly from the sale of the engraving to be made from it, and finally from the sale of the picture itself.

The Railway Station by W. P. Frith

The Illustrated London News, 2 March 1861

A daring robbery at the residence of Lady Otway, Brunswick Terrace, Brighton, took place yesterday se'nnight. The thieves not only removed all the valuables in the different rooms, but took a gold watch and appendages from the bed's head, and a diamond ring from off her ladyship's finger whilst she lay asleep. The property carried off is valued at £1700.

In contrast, a small item near the bottom of a column on 9 March may have taken his attention:

There has been a marked increase in pauperism in England and Wales.

━━━◦◇◦━━━

Tolstoy was to be greatly distressed by the human misery in the slums of Moscow when he took a house there twenty years later. On occasion the volume of suffering he saw reduced him to tears. One wonders what scenes he may have witnessed in the London of 1861.

It was not only in Russia that a whole section of society occupied the lower depths. Dickens was already doing for the underprivileged of England what Maxim Gorki would do in Russia forty years later. The sheltered children of a favoured class were privately tutored or went to university, grew up, had children of their own, and remained throughout their lives almost entirely oblivious of the nature of extreme poverty. Reform belonged on the whole to the realm of private philanthropy; reform of the prisons, the hospitals, the schools, and the appalling housing situation. Many people talked in general terms of the need for improvement; those who did anything about it were a small minority.

Most members of the middle class, whether in the upper or lower echelons of that stratum, valued the sense of self-congratulation which came from being a cut above those less fortunate. Whether one was a small shopkeeper in Hackney or a prosperous mill-owner living in Portman Square, once one's foot was on the social ladder the higher rungs beckoned enticingly. Marriageable daughters, virginal, trained in lady-like accomplishments and knowing how to order a household of servants, were a means to further elevation.

Increasing one's status by accumulating money was a stimulating business and an engrossing hobby. Possibly one's grandfather had been perspicacious enough to make certain right decisions in the days of the German Georges or Queen Anne, which had enabled him to obtain money, property and, above all, social standing, advantages his descendants now enjoyed by right. Though if one lived in that house in Portman Square one might perhaps prefer to be discreet about the origins of one's wealth. To be well-connected was the thing, to acquire a growing circle of well-off and influential in-laws. With the rich man in his castle and the poor man at the rich man's gate (outside, of course, not allowed in) and God in His Heaven, all was reasonably right with the world. Most of the prosperous were without a social conscience. It was not that they were callous; they simply disliked seeing filthy barefoot children begging in streets and squares which had pretensions to gentility. To preserve the admirable *status quo* it was essential that the poor remain segregated, and preferably out of sight. Out of smell, too, for the really disgusting thing about the poor was that they stank.

They were undeniably dirty; they were, presumably, hungry and their children's faces tended to be covered in sores. If you were not to have an uncomfortable conscience about them it was very easy to believe that they were also shiftless, lazy, and workshy, preferring to beg and to steal rather than do an honest day's work. If one was a good Christian (and of course one went to church every Sunday) one was not averse to giving a little charity on occasion to a deserving case. Always, however, at a distance; they might carry contagion.

Things were, by and large, excellently ordered; there were workhouses, orphanages, and asylums for the poor, and of course penal establishments for those in need of correction. There were even 'ragged schools' where their children could be taught to read the Bible and respect their betters.

Halfpenny Ices Tolstoy wrote 'When I see these dirty tattered children, with their bright eyes and angels' faces, I am filled with apprehension, as if I were seeing drowning people. How to save them? Which to save first? That which is drowning is that which is most valuable, the spiritual element in these children.'

The over-riding dread of those who had only recently achieved the rise to lower middle-class status was of a relapse into poverty. The pit out of which these had so painfully climbed was still there, waiting to engulf those unlucky or foolish enough to lose their footing. No skill as carpenter, bricklayer, or clerk could protect a man against sickness, injury or sudden death. Any of these

THE ILLUSTRATED LONDON NEWS.

No. 1078.—VOL. XXXVIII.]　　　SATURDAY, MARCH 9, 1861.　　　[WITH A SUPPLEMENT, FIVEPENCE

THE LATE OUTBREAK AMONG THE CONVICTS AT CHATHAM.

ST. MARY'S CONVICT PRISON : ARRIVAL OF THE MILITARY.

Our readers have been from time to time made acquainted with the riotous proceedings on the part of the convicts who are undergoing their sentences of penal servitude at the establishment on St. Mary's Island, Chatham ; and we now give some Illustrations in connection with the outbreak, which, happily, was quelled with but little loss of blood. On this dreary piece of swamp land called St. Mary's Island, where an extent of about 250 acres seems to produce little but dank, frowsy specimens of vegetation, rooted in the slimy mud and chalk which everywhere intersect the stagnant pools, employment is found

Report of the riots at St. Mary's Prison from *The Illustrated London News*

26

calamities could cause a workman and his family to drop below the poverty line into that stinking abyss.

There were, in this twenty-fourth year of Victoria's reign, several millions of her subjects living on or perilously close to the extreme poverty line. For these it was only a small step to actual starvation, and it was from among this section of society that the overwhelming proportion of the inhabitants of the gaols came. The penal system was harsh and degrading, breaking the weak and defenceless along with the vicious.

—⊷⬦⊶—

Vast numbers of people were caught in the poverty trap by the accident of birth, having themselves been born of destitute parents. There was only the thinnest of dividing lines between the lower middle class and the nightmare of utter penury. Housing conditions were intolerable in parts of London at the time of Tolstoy's arrival, and remained so long afterwards. In the congested courts and alleys sanitation was almost non-existent. Blocked communal privies overflowed, seeping into crowded cellars. The Royal Commission on Housing published a Report as late as the 1880s which was to reveal a situation which had existed without official comment for half a century: 'It seems no uncommon thing for the closets to be stopped and overflowing for months . . . in some parts of London they are used as sleeping places by the homeless.'[1]

There had been 13,000 registered deaths from cholera in London in 1849, and little had been done since to prevent further epidemics. Only the able-bodied could hope to survive into middle-age and even they were periodically destroyed in their thousands, if not by cholera then by typhoid, diphtheria, or scarlet fever. Other common causes of death in 1861 were tuberculosis, smallpox and starvation. Children were dying in greater numbers than ever before, largely as a consequence of the unprecedented overcrowding which hastened the spread of disease. Ailing infants stood very little chance against horrendous living conditions which were aggravated each winter by the misery of bitterly cold weather. From November until February an acrid yellow fog, due to the burning of sea coal, hung motionless in the narrow streets.

The cheerful cockney, looking on the bright side in adversity, blessed with a ready native wit, all winkles and jellied eels, disporting himself and his family on 'appy 'Ampstead at Bank Holidays, was at best a fair-weather phenomenon. Where he existed, he was not the poor; he had a trade, was perhaps a costermonger with a little money to jingle in his pockets.

The jovial poor were encountered only as low-life 'characters' in Victorian novels and plays. They were there as reassuring comic relief, and belong to the sentimental side of mid-nineteenth century fiction, in which a Merry Christmas was enjoyed even in the humblest of homes by the good, honest and, above all, harmless poor, whose kind hearts were more than coronets. This comforting fairy tale of what it was like to be poor concealed the shocking truth of real poverty. While those who accepted this picture sang sentimental ballads to the tinkling of pianos in ornately furnished drawing-rooms, large numbers of people endured a wretchedness compounded of malnutrition, ill health, and anxiety which is almost beyond our present day comprehension.

The reality behind the official statistics was the nocturnal presence of rats in large numbers, of fouled bedding infested with bugs and damp with urine, of lice in the hair, and the ever present stench of excrement. Syphilis, bronchitis, rheumatism, rickets, food poisoning, diarrhoea, and intestinal worms were so commonplace as to be taken for granted, inescapable facts of life.

The remarkable thing is not that so many of the poor died young during the mid-nineteenth century but that so many managed somehow to survive.

———◦◇◦———

In 1858 London had been alarmed by what became known as the Great Stink. The Thames was low, scarcely moving, heavy with filth of every kind, including the offal from the knackers yards of Lambeth and the Whitechapel slaughter-houses. Owing to the unrelieved heat of a long, rainless summer, the stench became so vile that it caused people to vomit. The gases rising from the scum on the river's surface were so obnoxious that Westminster Bridge could only be crossed with a handkerchief soaked in vinegar clasped to the face. The windows of the Houses of Parliament, tight shut in the blazing sunshine, had to be draped with heavy curtains impregnated with chloride of lime before the business of Government could continue.

Reformers had been trying for many years to introduce a co-ordinated drainage system to the capital. After much obstruction from those with vested interests, the Metropolitan Board of Works was formed, following the outcry which accompanied the Great Stink. With Joseph Bazalgette as chief engineer, work began at long last on the construction of a desperately needed Northern Outfall Sewer to conduct the effluent downriver to Barking Creek. This and other similar projects were the beginnings of an overall plan to replace with wide, cast-iron pipes the crumbling brick and wood sewers which dated back to the reign of Charles the Second.

Cheap fish at St. Giles

In 1861 Henry Mayhew produced an extended second edition of his *London Labour and the London Poor*. The first edition had appeared in 1851, and had jolted a little the complacency of a society congratulating itself on the success of the Great Exhibition in Hyde Park. The 1861 edition contained even more detailed accounts of the wretched lives of the children and old people who eked out a miserable existence by such occupations as picking up the 'pure' (i.e. dogs' droppings) from the streets, which they sold for a few coppers a bucketful to be used for the curing of leather. Other destitute children still scavenged for anything of value in the black mud of the river and among the rats and ordure in the old wooden sewers.

The previous few decades had seen a phenomenal growth in the population of the slums. To the continuing influx into London from the countryside were

Fleet Street in 1863

An engraving of 1874 showing the Model Lodging-Houses, Columbia Square, Bethnal Green, executed by Baroness Burdett-Coutts.

added large numbers of penniless immigrants, fleeing from famine in Ireland and from the anti-Jewish pogroms in Eastern Europe. In *Dombey and Son* Dickens wrote of those who came to London, footsore and weary, hoping for a new life, gazing in fear at the great smoking city before them from the surrounding hills. 'Food for the hospitals, the churchyards, the prisons, the river, fever, madness, vice and death, they passed on to the monster. . . . and were lost.'[2]

In spite of the high mortality rate, the numbers of the poor continued to increase. By the time of the census of 1861 they had reached unmanageable proportions. As the tide spread, with its attendant disease and filth, it seemed to the alarmed inhabitants of the neighbouring areas as if a human cesspool was threatening to overwhelm them.

What Pevsner calls 'the immeasurable vastness of London's slums'[3] was by no means confined to the East End. There were many sprawling and congested areas well to the west of Aldgate Pump without sanitation or any organised system of refuse disposal and the removal of night soil. It was in an attempt to break up these areas that there were cut through them in the 1850s and 1860s, such thoroughfares as New Oxford Street, Holborn Viaduct and Rosebery Avenue.

A contributory factor to the growth of the slums was that formerly pleasant areas all over London were being transformed in the space of a few years by the construction of railway termini. South of the Thames, Battersea Station, later renamed Clapham Junction, was built in 1845, and as a result the population of Battersea had quadrupled by 1861 from five to twenty thousand. The village atmosphere of the riverside districts of Battersea, Wandsworth, and Lambeth was largely destroyed by the construction of rows of meanly-built, back-to-back, terrace houses for those who earned their living on or by the railways. These insanitary dwellings remained until the areas were redeveloped, piecemeal, in the decade of prosperity which preceded the First World War.

A few public-spirited philanthropists were endeavouring to tackle the housing problem where conditions were at their worst; in the East End itself. In the year of Tolstoy's arrival, the first large-scale blocks of flats for the labouring classes were being erected in Bethnal Green at the expense of the Baroness Burdett-Coutts. Stark barracks though the new tenement blocks were, with asphalt yards and no blade of grass to be seen, they were hailed by Dickens and Lord Shaftesbury as a vast improvement on the rat-infested warrens which they replaced. The problem, however, remained. Here and there the old insanitary alleyways were demolished, supplanted by the new style buildings, but the slums continued to spread.

Gladstone, centre, at Edgware Road station on 24 May, 1862, during the first trial trip on the new Underground

Tolstoy's energy and enquiring mind must have made him the most insatiable of sightseers, in London as in the other cities he had visited. The world's first underground railway, constructed by the cut-and-cover method along what is now the Euston Road, would be opened in 1863, to run between Paddington and Farringdon Street. On the opening day, thirty thousand passengers would venture upon the unprecedented journey beneath the roadway. The work was in full swing in the March of sixty one, and Tolstoy may well have been among those who stopped to watch the navvies running their heavy laden wheelbarrows up swaying planks to the embankment.

England now had an engine at its heart. Factory chimneys covered much of the landscape like an ugly belching forest. One senses everywhere a desperate teeming vitality, an urge to survive, to better oneself while one's strength lasted.

It was a time of extraordinary contrasts, containing the first faint glimmerings of the twentieth century to come, and yet still in some ways the England of the Hanoverians and the seventeen hundreds. On the one hand the underground railway, and on the other the chilling fact that public hangings were not abolished until 1868.

Tolstoy's Visit

While in London Tolstoy met Alexander Herzen, the Russian socialist and political writer, who had been living in exile in England since 1852, and saw him almost every day. Herzen wrote to Turgenev, giving him his impressions of Tolstoy, whose writing he had praised in his magazine *The Bell* but whom he had not hitherto met.

> I am seeing a great deal of Tolstoy. We have quarrelled. He is stubborn and talks nonsense, but is naïve and a good man.[1]

Herzen's daughter Natalya later recollected Tolstoy's first visit. She was only a small child but had read *Childhood* and had loved it. She was also more than a little ready to be ènamoured of its author, who was still quite a young man, she understood, and the hero of Sevastopol.

Hearing that Tolstoy was coming, she asked permission to be present. At the appointed hour she sat waiting in a chair in a corner of her father's study, still and silent so as not to be observed. The servant announced the arrival of Count Tolstoy. Her heart beat rapidly. She expected to see a grown-up extension of the sensitive boy he had written of with such understanding. Instead, to her disappointment, there entered a man dressed in the latest fashion, who began to talk enthusiastically to her father about prize fights, of which he had apparently seen a great many since arriving in London. In later life she recalled wistfully that not one word did she hear which came up to her expectations of what she had imagined him to be.

It's not unlike a scene from *Childhood*. The little girl, wide-eyed, silent, watchful, her own thoughts unspoken in the presence of the grown-ups.

LONDON, TUESDAY, MARCH 12, 1861.

SACRED HARMONIC SOCIETY, Exeter-hall —Conductor, Mr. COSTA.—The usual Passion Week performance of the MESSIAH will take place on Wednesday, March 27. Principal vocalists—Miss Louisa Pyne, Madame Sainton-Dolby, Mr. Sims Reeves, and Mr. Santley.

Tickets, 3s., 5s., and stalls, 10s. 6d. each (for which early application requisite), at the Society's office, 6, in Exeter-hall.

Cheques or post-office orders to be made payable to Mr. James Peck, crossed "Coutts and Co."

CRYSTAL PALACE.—THIS DAY (Tuesday), and daily during the week (Saturday excepted), the LONDON GLEE and MADRIGAL UNION (under the direction of Mr. Land), Miss J. Wells and Miss Eyles, Mr. Baxter, Mr. W. H. Cummings, Mr. Land, and Mr. Lawler, will give their popular and eminently successful ENTERTAINMENT, interspersed with Remarks and Anecdotes, by Thomas Oliphant, Esq. (Literary Illustrator). The programme this day will include the following glees, madrigals, and old ballads :— "Away to the Summer Woods"—Coward. "There is beauty on the mountain" J. Goss. "When the wind blows"—W. Horsley. "Sleep, Gentle Lady" Bishop. "All creatures now"—J. Bennet. "In the merry spring"—A.D. 1613. "May-pole Song and Chorus"—A.D. 1670. "Down in a Flowery Vale"—1529. "Come, here's to Robin Hood"—17th century. "O, bid your faithful Ariel fly"—Thomas Linley, jun. Ancient Wooing Song, "I have House and Land in Kent"—A.D. 1613. "Near Woodstock Tower"—Traditional, &c. The Crystal Palace orchestra, conducted by Mr. Manns, will accompany "O, bid your faithful Ariel fly," and "Sleep Gentle Lady." Open at 10. Orchestral performance at 1. Entertainment at 3. Concluding with performance on the Great Festival Organ by Mr. W. J. Westbrook. Admission 1s. ; children under 12, 6d.

CRYSTAL PALACE.—Mr. HENRY BAUMER will perform his PIANOFORTE CONCERTO in B Minor at the next Saturday Concert, March 16.

MR. CHARLES DICKENS will READ, Thursday evening, March 14, at St. James's-hall, Piccadilly, his CHRISTMAS CAROL and the BOOTS at the HOLLY TREE INN, and on Friday evening, March 22, his Story of Little Dombey and the Trial from Pickwick. Stalls, 4s. ; balconies and area, 2s. ; back seats, 1s.—at Messrs. Chapman and Hall's, 193, Piccadilly ; and of Mr. Austin, ticket-office, St. James's-hall.

LAST WEEK of MR. WILLIAM STANLEY's "SEVEN AGES of WOMAN," every evening, at 8 at the Egyptian-hall, Piccadilly (except Saturdays). Saturday, at 3. Stalls, 3s. ; area, 2s. ; gallery, 1s. Stalls can be secured at Mr. Sams', Royal Library, 1, St. James's-street.

LAST NIGHT but THREE of Miss GRACE EGERTON's (Mrs. George Case) highly successful entertainment, LATEST INTELLIGENCE. Received with enthusiastic laughter and applause. THIS EVENING, at 8, at the Bijou Theatre (Her Majesty's Concert Room), Her Majesty's Theatre. Pit, 1s. ; boxes, 2s. ; stalls, 3s. ; private boxes, one guinea. The last morning performance on Saturday next, at 3.

MR. and Mrs. GERMAN REED, with Mr. JOHN PARRY, TO-NIGHT, in their popular ENTERTAINMENT, and every evening except Saturday, at 8, Thursday and Saturday afternoons, at 3, at the Royal Gallery of Illustration, 14, Regent-street. Unreserved seats, 1s., 2s. ; stalls, 3s. ; stall chairs, 5s. ; secured at the Gallery, from 11 to 5, and at Messrs. Cramer, Beale, and Co.'s, 201, Regent-street. The last two weeks of the present entertainment.

MR. W. S. WOODIN's NEW ENTERTAINMENT, the CABINET of CURIOSITIES, at Polygraphic Hall, King William-street, Charing-cross, TO-NIGHT, and every evening (except Saturday), at 8. Private boxes, £1 1s. ; stalls and box stalls. 3s. ; area, 2s. ; amphitheatre, 1s. A plan of the stalls may be seen,

Dickens in 1861, from an engraving by Edward Stodart

The item of most interest to Tolstoy from *The Times* of 12 March 1861, the day of his visit to St. Marks, would undoubtedly have been the announcement of Dickens's reading at St. James's Hall.

Dickens was sixteen years older than Tolstoy, and his creative achievement was at its height while Tolstoy's was only just beginning. He had been extremely popular in Russia for almost twenty years, and Tolstoy had long been one of the most enthusiastic of his admirers. The March copy of *All the Year Round*, containing the latest instalment of *Great Expectations*, was very likely to have been on Tolstoy's reading list while in London.

Tolstoy frequently disparaged his own work but was almost always generous in his appraisals of other writers. Dickens was, he considered, a genius born once in a hundred years, and a far greater writer than himself. A portrait of Dickens hung in his study at Yasnaya Polyana. In 1852, nine years before he came to England, he had written in his diary 'How delightful *David Copperfield* is!'[2] The Russian translation had appeared in 1851. As an old man he was to write 'Dickens interests me more and more. I have asked Orlov to translate *A Tale of Two Cities*, and I will ask Ozmidov to do *Little Dorrit*. I would undertake *Our Mutual Friend* myself if it were not that I have something else I have to attend to.'[3] He listed a number of other books by Dickens which he had enjoyed; among them were *Pickwick Papers*, *The Old Curiosity Shop*, *The Mystery of Edwin Drood*, and *Oliver Twist*.

But *did* Tolstoy, as all his biographers have stated, hear Dickens 'lecture on education' while in London? This has always been reported as an undisputed fact, based upon a remark he made to a friend some forty years later. 'I have seen Dickens in a large hall. He was lecturing on education.'[4]

In endeavouring to discover where this lecture took place, I came up against the fact that the Dickens Society has no record of Dickens *ever* having lectured on education. During the Spring of 1861 he gave six readings from his works at the St. James's Hall in Piccadilly. His only public engagement during the time Tolstoy was in London was the reading advertised in *The Times* of Tuesday 12 March and given on the evening of the following Thursday. It seems certain that this was the occasion referred to by Tolstoy. It is extremely unlikely that Dickens also gave an unadvertised lecture on education 'in a large hall' and that this has gone completely unrecorded. Possibly Tolstoy's words, long after the event, have been misquoted.

There is another explanation. He had been for years an ardent Anglophile and an avid reader of English literature, who could also speak the language with tolerable fluency. He was, however, as he later observed, unpractised at that time in the more difficult business of understanding spoken English. Dickens may well, in the course of that evening, have made some incidental remarks from the platform about education. These could perhaps have seemed to Tolstoy so valuable that they may have assumed an overriding importance in his subsequent recollection of the occasion.

Tolstoy later spoke of having attended the House of Commons, where he heard Palmerston deliver a speech. He found him 'boring and meaningless'. The occasion would appear to have been on Monday 11 March, the day before he went to St. Mark's. The speech was reported in the following Saturday's *Illustrated London News*, 16 March 1861.

> [Lord Palmerston] said that the policy of France for some years had been to get a navy equal, or superior, to that of this country. He did not blame her for that, but he held that we ought to maintain our naval supremacy if it were only to protect our colonies and our outlying trade. . . . In his opinion there was no possibility of maintaining friendship between two great, powerful, and wealthy nations, unless they were each in a position of defence. . . . Our Navy was no doubt the finest in the world, but it was deficient in iron-plated ships, and in this respect it was necessary that we should strengthen ourselves.

One of the sights most eagerly anticipated by male visitors to London was that presented in the Haymarket after dusk. With the lighting of the gas lamps there began the regular promenade of the ladies of the town, overflowing from the crowded pavements into the roadway. This was the permissive underside of Victorian London. Prostitutes of every age strolled among the throng of sightseers, customers, and missionaries distributing tracts.

If Tolstoy was there as an observer, or indeed in any other capacity, he left no record of his impressions. But only the following year his countryman and fellow writer Dostoevsky found it an unforgettable experience and wrote of it in his *Summer Impressions*.

> . . . on Saturday nights half a million working men and women and their children spread like an ocean all over town, . . . and . . . guzzle and drink like beasts to make up for a whole week . . . Crowds throng the open taverns and the streets. . . . The beer houses are decorated like palaces . . .

Anyone who has ever visited London must have been at least once in the Haymarket at night. It is a district in certain streets of which prostitutes swarm by night in their thousands. Streets are lit by jets of gas – something completely unknown in our own country. At every step you come across magnificent public houses, all mirrors and gilt . . . You will find old women there and beautiful women at the sight of whom you stop in amazement. There are no women in the world as beautiful as the English.

The streets can hardly accommodate the dense, seething crowd. The mob has not enough room on the pavements and swamps the whole street. All this mass of humanity . . . hurls itself at the first comer with shameless cynicism. Glistening, expensive clothes and semi-rags and sharp differences in age – they are all there . . .

In the Haymarket I noticed mothers who brought their little daughters to make them ply that same trade. Little girls, aged about twelve seize you by the arm and beg you to come with them. I remember once amidst the crowd of people in the street I saw a little girl, not older than six, all in rags, dirty, barefoot and hollow-cheeked; she had been severely beaten, and her body, which showed through the rags, was covered with bruises. She was walking along, as if oblivious of everybody and everything, in no hurry to get anywhere, and Heaven knows why she was loafing about in that crowd; perhaps she was hungry. Nobody paid any attention to her. But what struck me most was the look of such distress, such hopeless despair on her face that to see that tiny bit of humanity already bearing the imprint of all that evil and despair was somehow unnatural and terribly painful. She kept on shaking her tousled head as if arguing about something, gesticulated and spread her little hands and then suddenly clasped them together and pressed them to her little bare breast. I went back and gave her sixpence. She took the small silver coin, gave me a wild look full of frightened surprise, and suddenly ran off as fast as her legs could carry her, as if afraid that I should take the money away from her.[5]

—◇◇◇◇—

Education in England

During the early years of the nineteenth century there had been two celebrated pioneers of education for the children of the poor. Their influence was great, though of doubtful benefit, and it lasted for over fifty years. The education of the new population of children in the manufacturing towns had got off to a very questionable start with the introduction of the Lancasterian or 'monitorial' method. 'A new and mechanical system of education', Joseph Lancaster proudly announced, 'invented under the blessing of Divine Providence.'[1]

Lancaster, a Quaker, had also devised a whole sequence of ingenious punishments to go with this divine and providential method of driving home relevant facts to the exclusion of all else. Relevant, that is, to the mechanical and soulless work in the factories for which the children were destined.

These were not, at least not initially, the sickly young of the slums. They were mostly the first urban generation from country stock, their parents having been unemployed farm workers who had come to the expanding factory towns in search of regular employment, however back-breaking. The children were born to earn their keep, and such education as they were given was very much designed to an end.

Lancaster's punishments included the use of leg-irons, handcuffs, and cages in which offenders were drawn on pulleys up to the roof. Boys were disciplined by being tied to a pillar, in the precise manner in which St. Sebastian was shown in pictures of the agonies of the saints. Lancaster claimed to love all children, and maintained that his principles made him incapable of ever inflicting physical pain. This refinement of spirit presumably also prevented him from perceiving the damage his system inflicted upon impressionable young minds. He introduced into his schools a structure of ranks distributed among a hierarchy of monitors. His schools were administered by petty tyrants chosen from among the children themselves, and the meek were victimised by the unscrupulous. Selected monitors were personally trained by him to be teachers and carry on his system. This was, in effect, the beginnings of teacher

Joseph Lancaster from a portrait by Hazlitt

training in England. Some of his maxims, which had to be chanted by the children in unison, passed into the language – 'A place for everything and everything in its place' He demanded immediate obedience to those he set in authority, and permitted no questioning of orders given.

In a Manchester school using Lancaster's method of inculcating hard facts and nothing else, a thousand children were taught simultaneously in a vast hall, controlled by monitors with the power to report offenders for punishment by monitors-general. The system of teaching was based on the question and concerted answer method borrowed from the church catechism. Blocks of facts were drummed into tired brains by a form of military drill. Shouted questions had to be followed by the prescribed answers chorused from a thousand throats. That the attempt to train children like robots was also being practised in other countries is borne out by Tolstoy's notes of what he saw in Marseilles. The reasoning behind this inhuman forcing was that any tendency to self-assertion in the children must be broken, that they must be made obedient to authority, and lose the ability to think for themselves. Those boys who did not find work in the factories or the mines were funnelled into the army, already conditioned to accept its tradition of unquestioning obedience enforced by flogging.

Lancaster was a tireless propagandist for the effectiveness of his methods and he received the support, both moral and financial, of wealthy landowners and politicians. Poor, half-mad George the Third promised him his patronage, adding with tears in his eyes 'It is my wish that every poor child in my dominions should be taught to read the Bible.'[2]

Dinner time at Greenwich Royal Hospital School

With these Royal words enshrined in his charter there was no holding Lancaster. Hot-tempered, spendthrift and markedly lacking in self-control, he became obsessed with a sense of Divine mission, and intensified the strict application of the Lancasterian method and the Lancasterian punishments. He was given enthusiastic backing by the mill-owners and the gentry, who were sometimes one and the same, and he was praised in glowing terms as a benefactor of mankind by the influential *Edinburgh Review*. A long and impressive list of eminent supporters was published, headed by the names of the entire Royal family. The considerable personal debts he had accrued were discreetly paid off by those who saw a practical value to the country stemming from his methods. Control and discipline were safeguards against revolution.

There were direct links between the chastisement inflicted in Lancaster's schools and the disciplining of children in some of the factories to which they were consigned. Among the schoolroom punishments they adopted was the use of 'the log'. This was a heavy baulk of wood which was tied to a child's neck as the penalty for talking. It caused severe pains in the neck, head, and spine.

A school in the East End of London using the Monitorial System with older boys passing on instruction to their juniors. The toys hanging from the rafters were rewards to be won with good marks.

Lancaster was vehemently opposed by the leaders of the established Church. The point at issue, however, was not the effects of his methods upon the children, but that the wholesale education of the young poor ought not to be in the hands of a member of a Nonconformist sect. It should instead be under the absolute control of the Church of England.

Just as in Russia, there were still many in England who believed the lumpen masses to be incapable of assimilating anything beyond the most rudimentary education, and who thought it unwise and dangerous to tamper with their ignorance. Civilised society, with its hierarchical layers of inter-dependence, had always functioned by the acquiescence of an illiterate proletariat. How far beyond religious instruction should the gates of knowledge be opened to them? It was felt that there had to be an entirely different kind of education for the poor, much more limited than that available to pupils from a higher level of society.

In his own eyes Joseph Lancaster was a God-fearing man with practical answers to pressing needs. No totalitarian state of more recent times ever thought up a more thorough method of breeding factory fodder from a subject people. What the children received was not education but brainwashing on a massive scale, calculated to make them useful to Society, and subservient to God, the King, their Country, and those set in authority over them. Fortunately England was not a totalitarian state. Among the Victorians were some who responded to Dickens' devastating condemnation in *Hard Times* of such experiments. The opening chapters of that book are no fiction. What Dickens describes there had already been in operation for many years when he sat down to write of Gradgrind and M'Choakumchild.

> Now, what I want is, Facts. Teach these boys and girls nothing but Facts. Facts alone are wanted in life. Plant nothing else, and root out everything else. You can only form the minds of reasoning animals upon Facts: nothing else will ever be of any service to them ... Stick to Facts, Sir!

> The scene was a plain, bare, monotonous vault of a schoolroom, and the speaker's square forefinger emphasized his observations by underscoring every sentence with a line on the schoolmaster's sleeve. The emphasis was helped by the speaker's square wall of a forehead, which had his eyebrows for its base, while his eyes found commodious cellarage in two dark caves, overshadowed by the wall. The emphasis was helped by the speaker's mouth, which was wide, thin, and hard set. The emphasis was helped by the speaker's voice, which was inflexible, dry, and dictatorial ...

> 'In this life, we want nothing but Facts, Sir; nothing but Facts!'

> The speaker, and the schoolmaster, and the third grown person present, ... swept with their eyes the inclined plane of little vessels then and there arranged in order, ready to have imperial gallons of facts poured into them.[2]

The speaker is Mr. Gradgrind, the schoolmaster Mr. M'Choakumchild, and the third person is referred to by Dickens only as a government officer. In the second chapter, headed 'The Murder of the Innocents', this government officer puts a question to the class.

> 'Would you paper a room with representations of horses?'

> After a pause, one half of the children cried in chorus 'Yes, Sir!' Upon which the other half, seeing in the gentleman's face that Yes was wrong, cried out in chorus 'No, Sir!' — as the custom is, in these examinations. 'Of course, No. Why wouldn't you?'

> 'I'll explain to you, then,' said the gentleman, after another and a dismal pause, 'why you wouldn't paper a room with representations of horses. Do

you ever see horses walking up and down the sides of rooms in reality – in fact? Do you?

'Yes, Sir!' from one half. 'No, Sir! from the other.

'Of course No' said the gentleman, with an indignant look at the wrong half. 'Why, then, you are not to see anywhere, what you don't see in fact . . . Now, I'll try you again. Suppose you were going to carpet a room. Would you use a carpet having a representation of flowers upon it?'

There being a general conviction by this time that 'No, Sir!' was always the right answer to this gentleman, the chorus of No was very strong. Only a few feeble stragglers said Yes: among them Sissy Jupe.

'Girl number twenty,' said the gentleman, smiling in the calm strength of knowledge.

Sissy blushed and stood up.

'So you would carpet your room . . . with representations of flowers, would you. Why would you?' said the gentleman. 'Why would you?'

'If you please, Sir, I am very fond of flowers' returned the girl. 'They would be the pictures of what was very pretty and pleasant, and I would fancy —'

'Ay, ay, ay! But you mustn't fancy,' cried the gentleman . . . 'You are never to fancy . . . Fact, fact, fact! . . . You are to be in all things regulated and governed . . . by fact. We hope to have, before long, a board of fact, composed of commissioners of fact, who will force the people to be a people of fact, and of nothing but fact.'[3]

—◦◦◇◦◦—

By 1810 Lancaster had promoted the establishment of fifty new schools in England. His system had crossed the Atlantic and was operating in New York, Philadelphia, Boston, and as far afield as Caracas in Venezuela. Quarrelling violently with the committee which his financial backers had appointed to administer his educational empire, he began to show all the symptoms of persecution mania. He complained bitterly of the trustees changing the name of his Lancasterian Society first to the Lancastrian Society and then to The British and Foreign Schools Society. He abused his supporters as well as his critics, and was several times imprisoned for debt. In 1818 he deserted England for the Americas, to extend the benefits of his system throughout the New World, living for several years in Venezuela and then in Montreal.

In 1833, at New Haven, in Connecticut, he published the last of his many pamphlets. It was incoherent, filled with self-congratulation and irrelevant Biblical texts.

EPITOME
OF SOME OF THE
CHIEF EVENTS AND TRANSACTIONS
IN THE
LIFE OF JOSEPH LANCASTER
CONTAINING AN
ACCOUNT OF THE RISE AND PROGRESS
OF THE
LANCASTERIAN SYSTEM OF EDUCATION AND
THE AUTHOR'S FUTURE PROSPECTS OF USEFULNESS TO
MANKIND
WRITTEN BY HIMSELF
AND PUBLISHED TO PROMOTE THE EDUCATION OF HIS
FAMILY

Of my Usefulness, I cast down all my Glory at the feet of Him who called me into being by His Power, Endowed me with Talents, and Redeemed me by His Blood.[4]

He met with a street accident in New York in October 1838, and died of his injuries.

———◁◇◁◇———

The other celebrated educationalist of the time was Andrew Bell. Born at St. Andrews in Scotland in 1753, he was the founder of the Madras system of education. He, too, was a hasty-tempered eccentric. The most marked feature of his character throughout his life was his love of money.

In 1774 he went to Virginia as tutor to a planter's family, and in 1787 to India as an army chaplain. Subsequently, he was appointed Superintendent of the Madras Male Orphans Asylum, which had been founded by the East India Company for the education of the half-caste children of military men. There he developed his system, which consisted of the then entirely novel idea of selecting individual children to give rudimentary instruction to the others, under the overall supervision of a master. Having gone out to India in impoverished circumstances, he had acquired the sum of £25,000 by the time he returned to England nine years later.

A number of schools were launched, based upon his system, and before long

Andrew Bell from the portrait by Owen, 1825

a heated enmity grew between Bell and his rival, Lancaster. The Madras system had the advantage in that it simplified the administration of a school by making very few actual teaching demands upon the staff. The amount of learning acquired by the pupils was minimal, but then it was generally held that it would be unwise to teach the children of the poor any more than was required to make them of use to society at the level at which it had pleased God to place them.

There would seem to have been little to choose between the two methods. Yet powerful forces were ranged on each side. There was a tug of war between the Dissenters and the Church of England over who should control the minds of the children of the masses. The bishops supported Bell against Lancaster the Quaker, and founded in 1811 the National Society for Promoting the Education of the Poor in the Principles of the Established Church. With Bell in charge, the number of its schools would rise in his lifetime to more than ten thousand.

He was a harsh despot, universally loathed and feared by all those who worked under him. His aim was to ensure that elementary schools were instructing machines, whose automatic functioning the teachers must do nothing to interrupt. They were to be rigidly administered, without the least deviation from a curriculum in which the imagination played no part.

For his services to education he received an honorary doctorate from the University of St. Andrews. He left a vast personal fortune of £120,000 to further his educational beliefs, and was buried with great honour and ceremony in Westminster Abbey.

The Lambeth Ragged School for Boys in 1846

The early nineteenth century had entertained great hopes of the benefits to be obtained from both Lancaster's strict monitorial and Bell's Madras systems.

By the mid-eighteen hundreds the limitations of the first had become undeniable, and it was only in the more backward parts of the United States that the system long continued. In 1846 the newly constituted Education Department recommended that monitors be replaced by student teachers, their abilities tested by examination, as a step towards the eventual staffing of schools entirely by fully-qualified adult teachers. It was the poet Southey who wrote of Lancaster, 'The good he has done is very great but only in the way that the devil has been the cause of the Redemption.'[5]

As for Bell's rival system, the Education Committee's Report of 1861, thirty years after his death, reported unfavourably upon it, noting that in schools using his Madras method, instruction was too inflexible and that not the least divergence from the limited objectives of its founder was permitted. The teachers were reported to be, not surprisingly, pedantic ignoramuses.

College of St. Mark, Chelsea, founded by the National Society for the Education of the Poor, 1843

Although the Government had accepted as far back as 1839 some degree of responsibility, in principle, for devising an overall system of national education for the children of the humbler classes, both finance and ideas still had to come from private individuals. Schooling would not be compulsory until 1880 and in the meantime the field was wide open to abuse by opportunists, though there were a few dedicated men who were able to offset to some degree the excesses of Lancaster and Bell. The task of educating the children of the poor continued to present many problems. After several generations of State-sponsored education freely available to all it is difficult for us today to visualise how fraught with conjecture and apprehension were the beginnings.

There was a desperate need for trained teachers. The unsuitability of most of those who taught the poor was a scandal which was only just beginning to come to light. They included bankrupt tradesmen who were themselves virtually uneducated and clerks who had lost their usual employment because of an addiction to drink.

It was to remedy this situation that a private body, the National Society for

Beside the Chapel attached to the College can be seen the octagonal Practising School. This engraving from 1843 emphasises the rural nature of the area.

the Education of the Poor, had founded the College of St. Mark, in Chelsea. Its two-fold aim was to train young persons as attached and intelligent members of the Church, and to prepare them to become teachers in Parochial and National Schools. What more sensible arrangement could there be than to build within the College grounds a 'practising' school, where the trainee teachers could gain experience by working with a ready supply of young pupils?

St. Mark's became one of the earliest teacher training colleges, its first Principal being a son of the poet Coleridge. The Revd. Charles Daymond, who had been one of the first intake of students to enter the College, was appointed Normal Master of the Practising School visited by Tolstoy. Its pupils were lucky enough to be enjoying an education of a different kind from that which the children at the Lancasterian and Madras schools had undergone.

12 March 1861

In the nineteenth century, the Russian Julian calendar was twelve days behind the Gregorian calendar used in England. The dates of letters and diary entries can give rise to confusion unless this is taken into account. Tolstoy left Brussels on Friday 1 March, by our reckoning, and arrived in London either that night or, more probably, on Saturday morning. He left again, for Paris, on Sunday 17 March.

While in London he obtained the following letter of introduction from Matthew Arnold, the poet, who was then a senior official in the Department of Education.

Education Department
Council Office,
Downing Street, London.

March 11th 1861

1. Abbey Street British School, Bethnal Green.
2. British School, Brentford, Middlesex.
3. Jews' Free School, Bell Lane, Spitalfields.
4. Minton Street Wesleyan School, Hoxton.
5. Perry Street British School, Somers Town.
6. British School, Stratford, Essex.
7. Wesleyan Practising School, Horseferry Road, Westminster.

I shall feel much obliged to the teachers of the above named schools, if they will kindly enable the bearer of this, Count Leon Tolstoy, a Russian gentleman interested in public education, to see their schools, and if they will give him, as far as they can, all the explanations and information which he may desire.

Count Leon Tolstoy is particularly anxious to make himself acquainted with the mode of teaching Natural Science, in those schools where it is taught.

Matthew Arnold[1]

Tolstoy in 1862, very much as he must have looked to the schoolboys of St. Marks

We know that Tolstoy visited the school in Chelsea, and he very probably did the rounds of those in Arnold's letter as well. Had he visited them ten years later it would have been as a celebrity, his fame as a writer having by then spread throughout the world because of the impact of *War and Peace*. In 1861 his visits to schools went undocumented . . . he was just another foreigner. My attempts to discover references to the visit of 'a Russian gentleman', named or otherwise, to the other schools have been defeated by a dearth of surviving records.

It was only five years since the British had won the Crimean War and that conflict was still fresh in the public's mind. Though with less accuracy on the part of the children than of their parents, judging from the cartoon which appeared in *Punch* on the day the former Russian artillery lieutenant arrived in London.

What Tolstoy was sent along to see at Chelsea in 1861 was a successful attempt at popular mass education, a great improvement on much that had gone before. The Department of Education wanted visitors from abroad to see the best that it had to show. The teaching staff were well-qualified, third year pupil teachers from the College, which had a high reputation. The children attending the Practising School were at this time mostly the sons of artisans, market gardeners, stable keepers, small shopkeepers and tradesmen. Many walked five miles to school and five miles back, summer and winter. Their parents paid fourpence a week and in those days it was the greatest bargain going.

SCENE.—PITT'S STATUE, HANOVER SQUARE.

STREET BOY. "*M, D, double C C, We, I—What does that mean?*"
STREET BOY, No. 2. "*Why, one o' our Rooshan Wictories this 'ere General won in the Crimea, stupid! Nobody can't pronounce the name.*"

The interior of the Practising School, 1846

They came to school from both sides of the river; from Hammersmith, Battersea, Wandsworth, Brompton, Putney, Kensington, Parsons Green, Fulham, North End, Notting Hill Gate and other districts. Approaching the school their way took them through areas where there were still extensive market gardens, watercress beds, and patches of only half-spoiled countryside. Fulham and Chelsea were, as they had been since Tudor times, the kitchen garden of London, provisioning the great 'mud salad market'[2] of Covent Garden. The only industries were brick-making and pottery.

As regards the date of Tolstoy's visit to the school, there is every reason to assume that it was on the same day the essays were written, 12 March, since he presumably collected them up and took them away with him. This was certainly what he did on a similar occasion elsewhere, as we shall see. The 12th was a Tuesday. The fine Spring weather of the previous week had broken, giving way to rain. *The Illustrated London News* of 16 March contains a reference to 'the glorious weather during the greater part of last week' and notes that 'Field labour has been checked again by the rain.' Hence the frequent references in the essays to rain, puddles, muddy ground and a hail storm.

The 1860s are insufficiently documented as regards popular education. We know what life was like at Rugby and similar schools for the privileged sons of gentlemen. From *Tom Brown's Schooldays* which was published in 1857 emanated the mystique of public school life. These first-hand accounts of a morning in the life of schoolboys at a much lower social level are something quite different. No member of Class 3B is a budding Samuel Pepys. Their essays are not very imaginative and are frequently repetitive. The writers, aged between ten and fourteen, are, however, refreshingly un-selfconscious. Prominent among these brief accounts of their interests is an enthusiastic obsession with playing marbles and with thumping each other. One feels somehow one knows them, recognises them from one's own schooldays . . . W. Hopwood, G. Lillywhite, Chalkley and the rest. One of the boys is somewhat unexpectedly named F. Drani. Where did his parents come from? From Central Europe perhaps, in the aftermath of the 1848 upheavals?

Essays is too grand a word; they are more like short letters, and one even begins 'Dear Sir . . .' Between them they give us a revealing, and oddly moving, picture not only of what these children were but of what they might grow up to be. You can feel the difference between them as individuals, sense their varied temperaments. Some are wags, one is a bit of a sneak, some are dull, others lively, and some are blessed with more enquiring minds than others. One has an eye for the girls, I suspect. Above all, one feels the energy which enabled them to survive in the free-for-all which was mid-Victorian London.

What did they subsequently do with their lives? They were fortunate in that they were a generation who would escape being minced in the War Machine. Just too late to be caught up in the Crimea, and far too late for the Napoleonic slaughter. Unless they enlisted and became involved in the Boer or Ashanti wars they were unlikely to die wearing uniform.

I think the visiting Russian gentleman must have enjoyed these artless essays written for him by the boys of Class 3B that day in Chelsea. Especially the one by Chalkley, who appears to have had a passion for gambling equal almost to Tolstoy's own at the card tables. For myself, being of an age to have experienced corporal punishment at school, the line which lingers most vividly down through the years is C. Raymond's 'Fortunately I just escaped having the cane which if I had not it would not have been very pleasant!'

26,22

Brodrick

Age 12 years

Composition

Me and Chakley came to school this morning and it was very dirty i had a game at marbles in which i lost but at play-time i won them nearly all back again.

At 10, o.clock we came into school and the first lesson was Scripture, after that came reading, and after that writing in copy books and then play. I told Stevens

a comb and he broke it all
up to peices. When we came
in from play we had latin
and music, then came dinner
i had a nice pie for dinner
and them came to school
again i had a game at
marbles and eggot i
then went in and washed
and then came in school
again.

_____

26,11

Chalkley
Age 12 yrs

Dear Sir.

When I came to school I played at marbles and lost all mine then we were called in and when we had had three lessons we came out to play again then I had some more marbles and lost them and then we went in and had Latin and Music and while we had Music there was a hail storm but when we came out to dinner it left off raining then

I bought some more marbles and

lost them then I played at egg-at

then we were called in school for

afternoon's work first we had

arithmatic and now we are having

composition which I like very

much

26.1

F. Drane
Age 14 and 3 mths
Class III

Composition

Dear Sir

I rose early this morning and felt just fit for school. I had my breakfast and came to school and the first lesson I had was scripture; I then had reading and was very much pleased with the subject, which was headed Volney Beckner. We next had Bookkeeping and then went to play for 1/4 of an hour We next came in and had Latin which I do not very much care about; we next had Music which is my favourite subject. I then went home and had my dinner and came back just in time for school where I had an Arithmetic

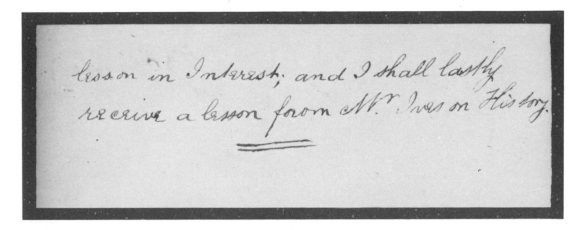

lesson in Interest; and I shall lastly receive a lesson from Mr. Ives on History.

Beaufort Place and Duke Street, circa 1870

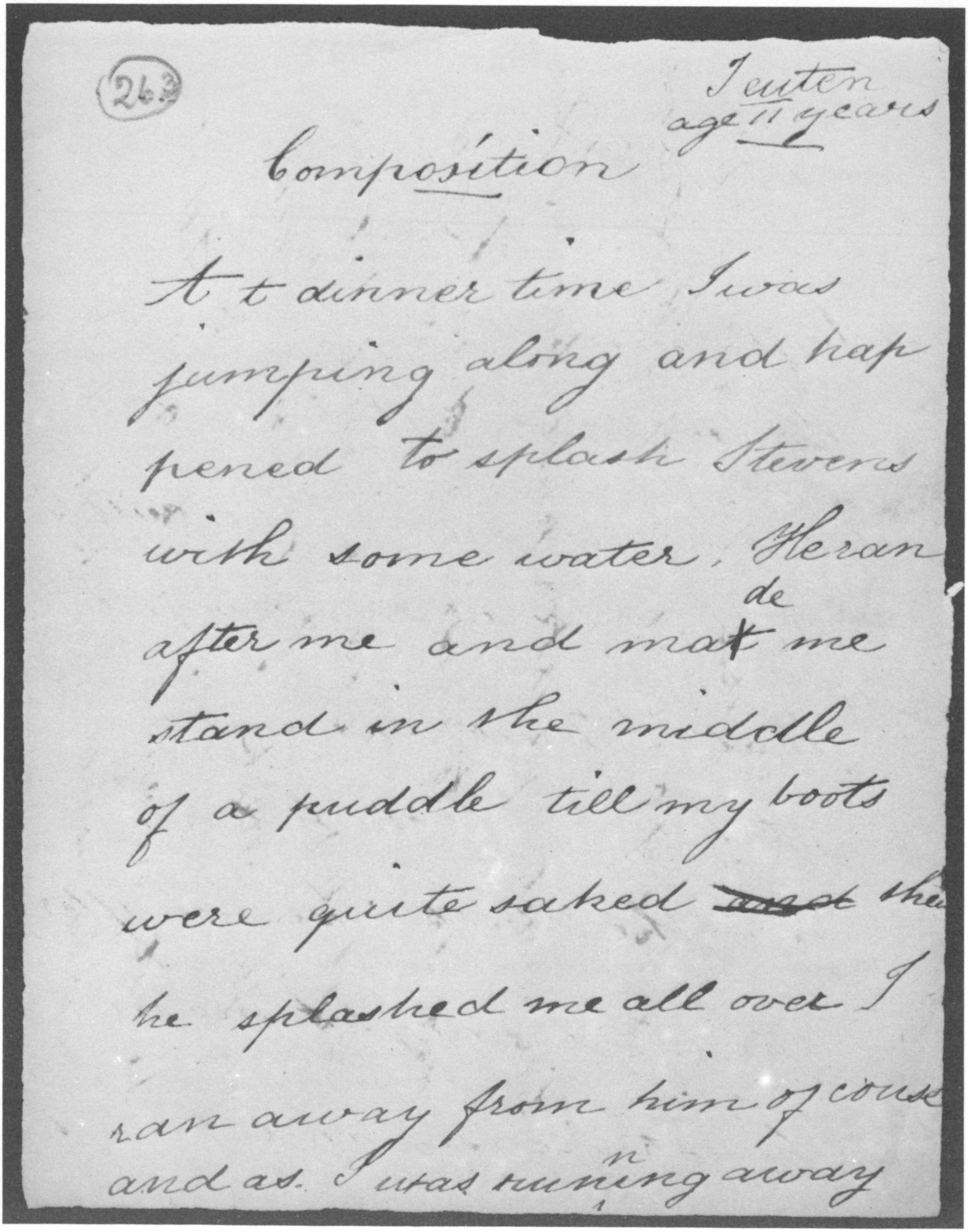

(26)

Leuten
age 11 years

Composition

At t dinner time I was
jumping along and hap
pened to splash Stevens
with some water, He ran
after me and ma*de* me
stand in the middle
of a puddle till my boots
were quite saked ~~and~~ she
he splashed me all over I
ran away from him of cousr
and as I was runing away

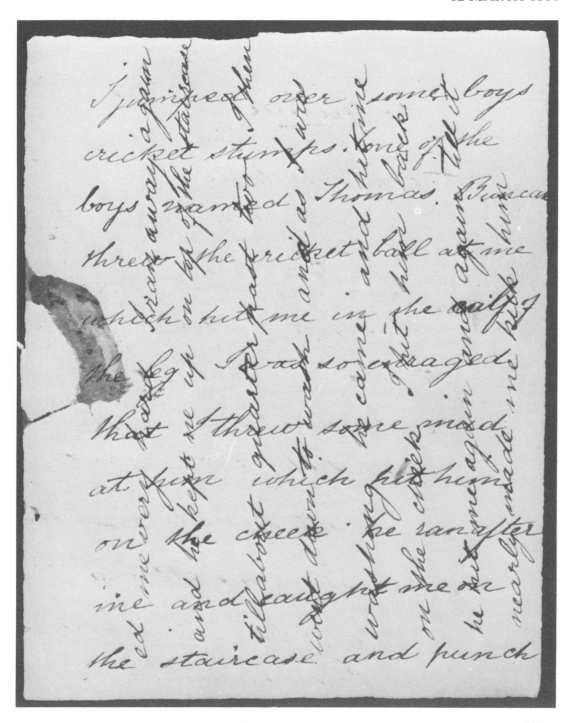

I jumped over some boys
cricket stumps. One of the
boys named Thomas Duncan
threw the cricket ball at me
which hit me in the calf of
the leg I was so enraged
that I threw some mud
at him which hit him
on the cheek. He ran after
me and caught me on
the staircase and punch

(26.2)

George Read
Aged 14 years
Class 3rd

Dear Sir

This morning before I had my
breakfast I was taking a coat from off a
nail & in under the coat was a weather
glass with some quick silver in it, and as
I was taken the coat off the weather glass
came of with it and fell on the floor all
smashed into pieces I began to pick up the
quicksilver with a piece of stiff paper. I
picked up so much as I could and when
I put it in my hand it ran out between
my fingers and it ran about on the table
just as if it were alive

A. Roffrey

(26,9)

Sir.

I started away at ½ past
8 oclock and got down
here at a ¼ past 9. and I
was too late for chapel
so I had a game with
my top and when I
I came in school I
had a lesson on scripture
after that reading
and. after that dictation.

Aged 12 years (26,12) W. King

When I came to school this morning it was raining. Raymond offered me a small broach for a shilling; it was gold and had twenty four pearls in it. I do not think he came by it honestly, because he told me yesterday that he found it in the Brompton Road, and to day that he had it given him. Lillywhite gave me some mustard seed which I threw into the fire. At a quarter past one I went home and *had my dinners;*

The corner of Danvers Street, Chelsea, circa 1870

Class III.

When I was coming to
School this morning
I met W. Garried against
Queen's Garden Buildi
and came to school with
him. When I got to
school I had my usual
lessons. We had music

3 Class   William Garrud

When I got up this morning I dressed myself and cleaned my boots and came to school. As I was coming I met Arthur, and Henry Bennett (but Bennet was sitting by me and says it is Harry) when I got to school I had a game with my top

Class. III: Charles Clarke.

Composition.

When I came out of my house
this morning I went &
called for Francis Hance Esq.
when I met some young
ladies who we know &
we went for a walk along
the water-side from Ham-
mersmith Suspension
Bridge to Putney and
then we went along
in a little boat from
one side to the other &
when we were about
the middle the boat

stuck fast in the mud, for
the tide was low, and a
man from the other side came
with another boat & took us
in it and when we had lan—
ded the young ladies left us
& then we came to school

Finis

C. C.

H. Johnson
Age 13 yrs

I started from home this morning at
about half-past eight and called for one
of my friends but as he was not very
well he did not come so I had to make
the best of my way alone. I paid my money
at the bridge and when I got over
                four
I saw ~~four~~ men removing some chalk
from one barge to another after stoping
here a few minutes ~~my~~ I walked up
Milmans Row which is not my usual

way when I came to the square I
waught one or two oranges and contented
myself by eating it

Lindsay House and Cheyne Walk, Chelsea, showing large, flat-bottomed Thames sailing barges.

26,14

Geo.d Upjohn, 6 III

A little Narative, Age 11 years

When I came to school this
morning I was rather late
so I had to go in directly.
The first lesson we had was
scripture, The second Reading
and the third Writing. We
then had a little play and
after that, Latin then we
practiced in the judas klas
Then came dinner and at
half-past two o'clock we were
again called in and then
we had for the sixth lesson

Arithmetic and the seventh *Composition*. As I played at nothing I have no more to say

From the Autho.

J.G. Glassbrook
Age 12

As I came to school, I did not notice any thing more than I usually do. I started from home at about half past 8 o'clock and arrived at school a little to late to go to chapel. The first lesson we had this morning was scripture (the history

of Joseph). The next lesson we had was reading. The next was writing in copy-books and then we went down to play. After coming up we began our Latin lesson. The last lesson we had was Music and when that was over

J Boorman
Age 12

Composition

This morning I got up at about seven o'clock and went for a walk as far as Fulham and back; then I had my breakfast, and went to school at nine. I was rather late for chapel and I played till ten, and then I fell in for school. We began by reading in the bible, the thirty seventh chapter of Genesis, which contains some part of the life of Joseph which is very interesting when we had finished that, we had reading. It was an account of Volny Bochner. and then writing

in copy books, and then we went down to play for a quarter of an hour, which was very nice. When we had come up we had Latin, I got good for my Latin, then I sang in the first music class before Mr Jaymond. After I had finished school for the morning I went home to dinner, I had a very nice one. I came back to commence school for the afternoon and gave the slates out and had arithmetic and got very good

(26.7)

W. Orpwood
Age 13 yrs

On coming to school this morning it was very showery I reached school this morning about ½ past 9 o'clock. After staying in the play-ground a short time the whistle was blown for to go in school and to commence lessons. The first lesson was Bible reading which occupied 3 qrs of an

hour after came reading in the 4 bks. After saying Latin we had Judas Maccabeus practising the chorus "Sing unto God" which occupied ½ an hour. After saying grace we were dismissed for an hour and ½. During that time I stayed in the playground seeing the boys playing at cricket marbles tops and buttons &c.

(26.8)

A Pitts
Age 12 yrs 4 days

Composition

It was about 9 o'clock this morning when I left home and my brother was with me. We had not gone far when we caught Henderson up with a few other boys but it is needless to relate all the little things however we got here in time. The first thing we had at was Scripture and we read

about Joseph this lesson lasted half an hour Then we had reading in the third irish book and next play for a quarter of an hour. We went in and had arithmetic and music and while we were singing it began pelting down with hail

Composition H. Rowland
12 years old

This morning I came quite a different
way to come to school on the side
I walked I saw two nice pictures on
glass. When I arrived in the yard
soon in school the first lesson was
in scripture and we read some of
the life of Joseph. The second
lesson was in writing in copy books,
in which I did not succeed very
well. After that I went down to
play. Then after play I went to do
my latin and declined gradus a step
After my latin I had music and after
that I went down to play. The

first thing I saw was some boys playing
at crickitt I soon began to play myself
and I ... one game of hide and
seek for a long time

A. Westbrook
years
Agr 10.10

Sir
When I first went
into school we had a
scripture lesson on the
life of Joseph when he
was in the pit and he
was sold to the Ismael
ites. And we had
reading and read
about Volney Beckny
a young Irish sailor
boy born at Londonster

and when he was 4 yrs
old he could swim a
distance of 12 miles.
then it was play from
11th to 12 o'clock and Latin
which we had to learn
about the Comparison
of Adjectives. After
we practised the chorus
with Mr Daymond
Sing unto God.
And then I had my
dinner.

Dictation

C. Raymond
Age 12 years 3 mo

This morning I was going to play at cricket with mast. Seaton but as it was so wet he did not bring his bat and ball so we could not play so I amused myself at seeing others play it it and then I went and played at peg top. And when I came into

shool the first lesson we had was scripture and we read the history of Jacob which was interesting indeed and after that we had latin which I did not quite know perfect but luckily I just escaped having the cane which If i had not it would not have been very pleasant.

Composition

W. Henderson
13 Years

A coming to school in the morning I did not see any thing of consequence. We came in school at ten oclock the first lesson we had was Scripture then Reading and Dictation then had half an hours play I did not play much on account of the ground being so muddy after our play we had Latin & Music after these lessons we dismissed for dinner it being about one oclock I had my dinner and had a game at marbles in a part of the playground called the covered playground at half past twelve we were called in by means of a whistle as

sion as this whistle was blown we all fell in under the covered playground and then marched up into school in order with our teachers we then had Arithmetic the sums which we worked were Compound Interest

Walter Henderson
March 12th
1861

(26.6)

H. Hall.
Aged 12 ys.

Composition.

The first lesson we had this morning
was Scripture and we read about
the history of Joseph which is very
interresting and I like it very much.
And the next was reading and
we read about Volney Beckner.
And the next was writing in copy
books. And then went out to play
and we had a good game at touch.

(26.19) Class III E Irish II

This morning I have been playing
at marbles I said my Latin,
and did my Arethmetic I have
seen them play at cricket I have
had a capital game with my
Top I saw a boy throw a stick
and hit a nother boy right in
the eye and made it all over
mud It has been a very wet day
I brought my dinner to day but
I generally have a hot dinner

(26.7)   Mercer
                         Class III
      Composition   Age 12 years 8 mths

I left home this morning about half
past 8, o'clock, the first lesson we had
this morning was Scripture we read
the 37 Chapter of Genisis. The next
lesson was reading then read about
Volney Beckner, after that we
had writing in Copy Books for
half an hour. Then we had a quarter
of an hours play

Class III   (26.?)   G. Lillywhite.
March 12th   Aged 13 5⁄6 years.

As I was coming to school
this morning I called for
A King; when I got to
school W. King and I had
a game. The first lesson
we had was scripture on
the life of Joseph. The
next lesson was reading,
it was about Volney Beck.

Fredk. Stevens
March. 12th 1860

As I was comming to School
this morning, I met with
a companion and then we
both hurried to get in time
for Chapel but unfortunately
were two late and then I
played about till it was time
to begin school. The first
lesson we had was Scripture.
the second was reading
and the third bookkeeping
which I enjoyed and then
came play after play came
Latin which I am alway
unfortunate and then

then came music which was
very amusing. At Last came
the dinner hour the hour and a
1/2 seemed very long because it
was very dirty and could not
play at any games then came
half pass four and then the wistle
blew that was to wash

Mr. H. Burrows
Composition. Class III rd.

I first had my breakfast and
afterwards prepared for school.
We had for the first lesson,
Scripture, and the next was
reading and afterwards writing
in copy books, we had play
for the next thing which
lasted for one quarter of an hour,
there were two more lessons
which were Latin and Music
and then we went home to
our dinner which I enjoyed
very much, and after my
dinner I left home for school
again this afternoon about two

o'clock and was in time
to have a little play before work.
The lessons for this afternoon
are Arithmetic, Composition
and History and we he have
Prayers and we go home.

The story of *Volney Beckner*, although belonging to the category of instructive moral tales, with an element of *Eric, or Little by Little* about it, could be enjoyed as an adventure story. No wonder it appears to have seized the imaginations of A. Westbrook, F. Drani, and the rest. If it sought to instil into them ideals of self-sacrifice (albeit under somewhat improbable circumstances) this in no way lessened their value as individuals.

In trying to trace the source of the tale I realised that it is very much a collector's item. Since I could find no record of it in England I applied to Trinity College, Dublin. The Assistant Librarian consulted the copy of *The Third Reading Book for the Use of Schools* but, alas, no trace of the elusive Volney.

In fact, A. Pitt's reference to the Third Irish Book was leading along a false trail. By fortunate chance a member of the Library staff had, in a private collection, a copy of *The Fourth Book of Lessons for the Use of Schools*, published 1859, and it was in this that Master Beckner finally came to light. I was subsequently able to trace it back to an earlier appearance in Chambers Miscellany for 1843.

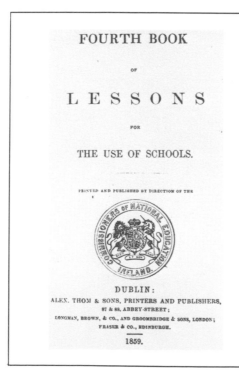

314   MISCELLANEOUS LESSONS.

When Volney was about nine years of age, he was placed apprentice in a merchant ship, in which his father appears to have sometimes sailed, and in this situation he rendered himself exceedingly useful. In tempestuous weather, when the wind blew with violence, tore the sails, and made the timbers creak, and while the rain fell in torrents, he was not idle at his post. The squirrel does not clamber with more agility over the loftiest trees than did Volney along the stays and sail-yards. When he was at the top of the highest mast, even in the fiercest storm, he appeared as little agitated as a passenger stretched on a hammock. The little fellow also was regardless of ordinary toils and privations. To be fed with biscuit broken with a hatchet, sparingly moistened with muddy water full of worms, to be half covered with a garment of coarse cloth, to take some hours of repose stretched on a plank, and to be suddenly wakened at the moment when his sleep was the soundest, such was the life of Volney, and yet he enjoyed a robust constitution.

Such was the cleverness, the good temper, and the trust-worthiness of Volney Beckner, that, at his twelfth year, he was judged worthy of promotion in the vessel, and of receiving double his former pay. The captain of the ship on board which he served, cited him as a model to the other boys. He did not even fear to say once, in the presence of his whole crew, " If this little man continues to conduct himself with so much valour and prudence, I have no doubt of his obtaining a place much above that which I occupy." Little Volney was very sensible to the praises that he so well deserved. Although deprived of the advantages of a liberal education, the general instructions he had received, and his own experi-

315   VOLNEY BECKNER.

ence, had opened his mind, and he aspired, by his conduct, to win the esteem and affection of those about him. He was always ready and willing to assist his fellow-sailors, and by his extraordinary activity, saved them in many dangers. An occasion at length arrived, in which the young sailor had an opportunity of performing one of the most gallant actions on record.

The vessel to which Volney belonged was bound to Port-au-Prince, in France, and during this voyage his father was on board. Among the passengers was a little girl, daughter of a rich American merchant; she had slipped away from her nurse, who was ill and taking some repose in the cabin, and ran upon deck. There, while she gazed on the wide world of waters around, a sudden heaving of the ship caused her to become dizzy, and she fell over the side of the vessel into the sea. The father of Volney, perceiving the accident, darted after her, and in five or six strokes he caught her by the frock. Whilst he swam with one hand to regain the vessel, and with the other held the child close to his breast, Beckner perceived at a distance, a shark advancing directly towards him. He called out for assistance. The danger was pressing. Every one ran on deck, but no one dared to go farther; they contented themselves with firing off several muskets with little effect; and the animal, lashing the sea with his tail, and opening his frightful jaws, was just about to seize his prey. In this terrible extremity, what strong men would not venture to attempt, filial piety excited a child to execute. Little Volney armed himself with a broad and pointed sabre; he threw himself into the sea; then diving with the velocity of a fish, he slipped under the animal, and stabbed his sword in his body up to the hilt. Thus sud-

316   MISCELLANEOUS LESSONS.

denly assailed, and deeply wounded, the shark quitted the track of his prey, and turned against his assailant, who attacked him with repeated lounges of his weapon. It was a heart-rending spectacle. On one side, the American trembling for his little girl, who seemed devoted to destruction; on the other, a generous mariner exposing his life for a child not his own; and here the whole crew, full of breathless anxiety as to the result of an encounter in which their young shipmate exposed himself to almost inevitable death to divert it from his father!

The combat was too unequal, and no refuge remained but in a speedy retreat. A number of ropes was quickly thrown out to the father and the son, and they each succeeded in seizing one. Already they were several feet above the surface of the water. Already cries of joy were heard—"Here they are, here they are—they are saved!" Alas! no—they were not saved; at least one victim was to be sacrificed to the rest. Enraged at seeing his prey about to escape him, the shark plunged to make a vigorous spring; then issuing from the sea with impetuosity, and darting forward like lightning, with the sharp teeth of his capacious mouth he tore asunder the body of the intrepid and unfortunate boy while suspended in the air.

Thus perished, at the age of twelve years and some months, this hopeful young sailor, who so well deserved a better fate. When we reflect on the generous action which he performed in saving the life of his father, and of a girl who was a stranger to him, at the expense of his own, we are surely entitled to place his name in the very first rank of heroes. But the deed was not alone glorious from its immediate consequences. As an

317   TERRIFIC INCIDENT.

example it survives to the most distant ages. When pressed by emergencies let us cast aside all selfish considerations, and think on the heroism of the Irish sailor boy—Volney Beckner.—*Chambers's Miscellany.*

LESSON XI.

TERRIFIC INCIDENT ON A MISSIONARY* VOYAGE IN THE SUNDERBUNDS.

THE Sunderbunds is an extensive tract of country to the south-east of Calcutta, stretching along the coast of the Bay of Bengal. It is composed of a number of creeks, all of which are salt, except those which communicate with the principal arm of the Ganges: these natural canals form a complete inland navigation. The passages through the Sunderbunds for large vessels are said to present a grand and curious spectacle—a navigation of more than 200 miles through a thick forest, divided into numberless islands by a multitude of channels, so various in width that a vessel has at one time her masts entangled among the branches of trees, and at another sails on a capacious river, beautifully skirted with woods. The waters (with the exception above mentioned) are every where salt; and the whole extent of forest is abandoned to wild beasts, so that they are seldom visited but in cases of necessity, except by wood-cutters and salt-makers, whose "dreadful trade" is exercised at the peril of their lives; for the tigers not only appear on the margin in quest of prey, but often in the night-time swim to the

---

* A missionary is one who is sent to preach the Gospel to the heathen nations.

Mrs. Iona Opie, who, along with her husband Peter Opie, has written a number of excellent and informative books on the subject of children's games, introduced me to that mine of fascinating information *Cassell's Book of Sports and Pastimes*, first published in 1881, which contains detailed accounts of the rules of Sunday Monday, Egg, and Eggot. Sunday Monday was presumably the game known variously as Days of the Week, Here Goes Up For Monday, Monday Tuesday Wednesday, etc. To quote from *Sports and Pastimes*:

> The game is to be played by seven boys or less, each boy . . . taking for his name that of one or more days of the week. The game must be played against the side of a house or a high wall, opposite to which the players range themselves. Sunday, as a general rule (though anyone may do so), then takes the ball, and throws it high against the wall, at the same time calling aloud the day-name of any one player, whose duty it is to catch the ball before it reaches the ground, the other players, in the meanwhile running away to a short distance, and ready to take a further run, should the ball not be caught by the player called. Upon the ball being duly caught, it is thrown by the catcher to the wall as before, the name of some other player being called, and so on again and again, so long as the ball is not missed. Should, however, any player, when called, miss the catch he loses a point or 'egg', as it is customarily termed, and he has to pick up the ball and throw it at one of the other players, all of whom will by this time have scampered away to a distance. If the ball hits any of them, that player also loses a point, and has to serve the ball, as at the commencement of the game. If, however, the ball, when thrown, hits no one, the player who missed the catch serves. Three eggs, or points, put a player out, the one last in being the winner, and he is the only one who administers, but himself escapes punishment, which, by the way, is not to hearty lads a very serious matter.
>
> The punishment inflicted is arranged in the following manner:– The last player out takes the ball, and leaning on his left hand, with his arm outstretched against the wall, throws the ball with his right hand as hard as he possibly can against the wall, sending the ball as far from the wall as his strength and skill can make it rebound. The winner then picks up the ball where it rests, and proceeding to a point straight in front of the loser, and at a distance from the wall equal to that at which the ball rested, is entitled to have three throws at the loser's right hand placed on the wall at a level with his shoulder, or should the loser prefer, he may take his punishment by turning his face to the wall, and letting the winner have three throws at his back. The winner is in this manner entitled to punish all the losers.[3]

I wonder who thought that up, in all its fiendish complexity, and with its somewhat sadistic 'punishment' to be inflicted by the winner on all the losers one by one at the end of the game!

Despite the references in Sunday Monday to 'egg', the name given to a lost point, the game of Egg, or Eggot, referred to by some of the boys is another game altogether, more correctly known as Egg Hat. *Sports and Pastimes* once again:

> This is a capital game for any number of lads up to a dozen or fifteen. It affords good sport in running and throwing. . . .
>
> Each boy places his cap against a wall, so that together the caps form a row, they being placed so as just to touch each other; a line at a distance of five or six yards from the row of caps should then be drawn, it being first seen that all the caps are so placed that a ball may readily be thrown, at the distance named, into any one of them. Some player is then selected to pitch, whose duty it is to throw the ball into any of the caps – for his own sake carefully avoiding his own. The owner of the cap into which the ball is thrown must immediately rush to the cap, snatch out the ball, and then do his best to throw the ball so as to hit one or other of his fellow players, all of whom will, of course, in the meantime, have made the best use possible of their legs to secure a safe distance. In the event of the ball striking any boy, a stone or pebble, called, and after which the game is named, an 'egg', is placed in his cap, and he takes the pitch. If, however, all are so fortunate as to escape being hit by the ball, then he who threw the ball scores 'one to the bad', in a similar manner, and himself has the task of proceeding with the pitch as first explained, and so on the game proceeds until some player scores three 'eggs' and has then to resume his cap, temporarily leaving the game, and is termed 'out'. The game then again goes forward until all but one, the winner, are out. . . . The winner may claim to punish the losers as is described under the heading Days of the Week.[4]

Buttons, as played by W. Orpwood, is not readily identifiable. Mrs. Opie thinks it may have been a game in which the boys aimed buttons into a circle, and had to lift out their winnings with the aid of a wetted thumb without dropping them. Or it might have been one in which they aimed a button against a wall and let it drop, hoping to hit a target button which lay on the ground.

There are a myriad of marble games. Among those listed in *Sports and Pastimes* are Bounce About, Bounce Eye, Eggs in the Bush, Picking the Plums and Teetotum Shot. No wonder that with such rich variety Chalkley and the others should have been engrossed to the point of mania with losing and winning their store of marbles. The essays don't specify which of the above or other marble games were favoured by the boys of the Practising School.

Sports and Pastimes gives some serious instruction in the art of playing marbles:

> All boys careful to do well that which is done at all should, before entering into any contested marble games, be quite satisfied that they thoroughly understand how to shoot a marble in the truly scientific and orthodox manner. There is only one way to shoot a marble properly. There may be plenty of ways never yet recorded . . . all of which should be unhesitatingly discarded in the higher marble games. . . . To shoot properly, correctly, and accurately, the marble is to be placed just above the first joint of the thumb of the right hand, and held there by the tip of the forefinger; the top of the thumb being firmly grasped by the middle finger, bent for the purpose . . . The aim is then to be taken, and the thumb let fly with such force as to shoot the marble away with the required speed. With practice great skill may soon be obtained. . . . In marble games, as indeed in all shooting practice, it should be remembered that the object aimed at is to be steadily looked at, its exact position being thoroughly taken in by the eye; the marble to be shot being firmly grasped by a hand in strict obedience to the brain of the shooter.[5]

Left A game of marbles, from a photograph taken in 1861. *Right* Old Battersea Bridge in 1874.

The bridge referred to in H. Johnson's essay would have been the old wooden Battersea Bridge, a structure of great character. Opened to foot passengers in 1771, and to carriages the following year. H.S. Simmonds in *All About Battersea*, published 1882, observes:

> In the severe winter of 1795 considerable damage was done to the bridge by reason of the accumulated ice becoming attached to the (timber) piles, and drawing them on the rise of the tide. . . . The bridge is 726 feet long and 24 feet wide. . . . In consequence of the serious hinderances which the structure caused to navigation on the Thames within the last few years, . . . strong iron girders have now [1882] been introduced. . . . In 1799 only one side of the bridge was lighted with oil lamps. In 1821 the dangerous wooden railing was replaced by a hand rail of iron, and in 1824 the bridge was lighted with gas, the pipes being brought over from Chelsea although Battersea remained unlighted for several years afterwards. . . . The bridge though convenient has an unsightly appearance unworthy of its position across a river spanned by some of the finest bridges in the world. At the foot of the Old Bridge is a toll-house . . . facing which is a painted board with charges for tolls headed 'Old Battersea Bridge Tolls By Act of Parliament 6° George III 1766'[6]

Not everyone agreed that its appearance was unsightly. It is more often referred to as 'much-loved' and 'picturesque', and it was painted by both Turner and Whistler. It was demolished in 1890 to make way for the present more prosaic structure.

Milman's Row, which H. Johnson walked along after crossing the bridge from the Battersea to the Chelsea side was more or less along the line of the present Milman Street, just west of Beaufort Street. His 'usual way' would presumably have been along Cheyne Walk and then Cremorne Road. The 'square' which he then reached, and where he bought the oranges, would appear to have been that area just to the north of the old Moravian burial ground. Here the straight line of the Kings Road is interrupted briefly by a sudden change of direction, where it may have widened slightly, before resuming its east-west progress. This kink in the Kings Road dates back to the days when it turned to avoid the wall of Beaufort House, which was demolished in 1740.

The Old Hammersmith Suspension Bridge, referred to by Charles Clarke was a remarkable feat of engineering, somewhat ahead of its time. It was in fact the first Suspension Bridge thrown across the Thames, and has been the subject of many attractive engravings and aquatints.

Designed by W. Tierney Clark, it was opened in 1827. It was of a simple but most impressive design, with two stone suspension towers having handsome arched entrances of the Tuscan order. Both Battersea and Hammersmith were toll bridges until 1880. Tierney Clark is buried in Hammersmith Parish Church and on his memorial slab is a representation of his beautiful bridge. An odd fact is that he subsequently made a European reputation by building an almost exact replica of his Hammersmith Bridge to span the Danube from Buda to Pest, where it can be seen to this day.

Left and right Hammersmith Suspension Bridge showing the toll booths

Queen's Gardens, where H. Bennett met W. Garrud, was a turning off the east side of Brompton Road, Knightsbridge. The Buildings referred to were in the Brompton Road itself, immediately to the north of Queen's Gardens. They consisted of a row of late eighteenth century terrace houses which had once possessed small front gardens. Many of the gardens had been built over to accommodate equally small flat-roofed single-storeyed shops. There were two cobblers, an apothecary, a solicitor, a draper, and so on. Number 8 was a grocer's shop which had been taken over not long before by Henry Charles Harrod, a wholesale tea merchant of Eastcheap.

Knightsbridge was by no means the fashionable area it would later become. Queen's Gardens had a particularly bad reputation, and after dusk it was dangerous to venture among the huddle of sordid alleys leading from it. Mr. Harrod's little shop in Queen's Gardens Buildings could not hope to attract the custom of well dressed ladies and gentlemen. These did their shopping at Fanny Heal's and Blundell Maple's establishments in the more select Tottenham Court Road or at Marshall and Snelgrove's in Oxford Street.

By the late 1860s the neighbourhood of the Brompton Road slowly began to change from a nondescript and somewhat unsavoury area into a modestly residential district; and Harrod started taking over some of the adjacent shops, laying the foundations of an empire to come, with a hosiers, a poulterers, and a shirt makers. Superimposing a street map of 1860 over one of today reveals that H. Bennett and W. Garrud met at what is now Harrod's main entrance hall.

87

TOLSTOY IN LONDON

It may be of interest to put alongside what we know of Tolstoy's descent upon St. Mark's on 12 March, the following recollection of one Julius Stoetrer, a master at a school he visited later in the month in Weimar.

On Good Friday [29 March] just as lessons began, at one o'clock, I . . . was about to commence teaching. A pupil . . . opened the door of the classroom and said, peeping in, 'A gentleman wants to see you.'

A gentleman followed without giving his name, and I took him for a German since he spoke as good German as any of us.

'What lessons are you going to have this afternoon?' he asked.

'History first, then German,' I replied.

'I am very glad to hear it! I have visited schools of Southern Germany, France and England; and should like to get acquainted with those of North Germany too.' . . . He produced his memorandum-book from his pocket and began hurriedly making notes . . . . When the lesson was over he asked 'What comes next?'

'I really intended beginning to read German, but if you prefer something else it can be changed?'

'I am glad of this. You see, I've pondered a good deal how to make thoughts flow fluently.'

I . . . tried to gratify him and asked the children to write a short composition. I named a subject, and the children had to write a letter on it in their copy-books. This seemed to interest the stranger very much, he walked between the benches, took up the pupils' copy-books by turns and tried to make out how they wrote and what about.

Not to distract the children I kept my seat. When the work was coming to an end, the foreigner said, 'Can I take these compositions with me? They are of the utmost interest to me?'

'That's a little too much' thought I, but told him politely that it was impossible. 'The children,' I said, 'have purchased their copy-books, and the price of each is six groschen; Weimar is a poor town, and their parents will be angry if they have to get new copy-books.'

'That can be overcome,' he said, and stepped outside.

I felt uneasy, so I sent a pupil to ask Herr Monhaupt, the headmaster and a friend of mine, to come to our class, as something unusual was taking place. Monhaupt came.

'You have played a nice trick on me,' said I. 'You have sent a queer fellow to me who wants to deprive the scholars of their copy-books.'

'I never did such a thing!' said Monhaupt.

'But,' I replied, '. . . he was brought to me by one of your pupils.'

Monhaupt recollected then that an official of importance had called at his place and told his wife that the gentleman who was accompanying him should be assisted in every way and shown everything.

In the meantime the stranger came back carrying a large package of writing paper . . . which he had bought in the nearest shop. When he came I had to introduce him to the director, and they exchanged credentials.

'Monhaupt, the director,' said the one.

'The Count Tolstoy, from Russia,' said the other.

So this was a Count and not a schoolmaster – a Russian who spoke German quite fluently.

We bade the children re-write their compositions on the sheets of paper that had been brought. Tolstoy collected all the sheets, rolled them up, and gave them to his servant, who was waiting outside.[7]

———◦◇◦———

On April 22nd he was in Berlin, and there he met Diesterweg, the Head of the Teachers Institute. He expected to find Diesterweg a man of enlightenment. Instead he proved to be, in Tolstoy's words, 'a cold heartless prig who thinks it possible to develop and guide children's souls by rules and regulations.'[8]

The next day, after nine months absence, he returned to Russia. He never went abroad again. He was dissatisfied with almost everything he had found in the schools of Western Europe during his lengthy tour of inspection. There is no record of his reactions to the school in Chelsea. We must hope that the obvious liveliness of the children there, under what seems to have been a fairly easy-going regime, commended itself to him. At Yasnaya Polyana he went his own way, following an even more independent line as a teacher than before.

———◦◇◦———

Return to Russia

He flung himself energetically into organising an educational system of an entirely new kind. Russia in the mid-nineteenth century was a blank slate as far as any real concept of education for the children of the peasant masses was concerned. It was on this blank slate that Tolstoy now proposed to write. He began training student teachers and greatly increased the number of schools under his control. He was concerned to establish not merely a theoretical but a practical method of teaching which, if widely adopted, could lift millions up out of the slough of ignorance.

His experience of schools in other countries had convinced him that the greater part of most people's education, in the true sense of the word, is obtained not from school but from life. Experience of life far exceeded in value anything acquired by the kind of schooling he had seen in half a dozen different countries. His own schooldays he remembered with distaste as an unhappy and largely wasted time. He believed, with burning certainty, that school need not be something separated from and inferior to life but a valuable part of the process of living.

It is a measure of the gulf which divided him from the official line that his views should have been considered revolutionary, positively dangerous to the established order. The authorities knew, before he left Russia, that he held that a State monopoly of education was undesirable. They were watchful, and highly suspicious of him, from the moment he returned across the Russian frontier. Informers were paid, and secret reports were prepared.

He held office for a time as a rural judge, and this facilitated his launching of no less than fourteen schools in the district, all under his personal supervision. In an article on education he described the Yasnaya Polyana school.

> The school is held in a two-storied stone building. Two rooms are given up to the school, one is a cabinet of physical curiosities, and two are occupied by the teachers. Under the roof of the porch hangs a bell with a rope attached to the clapper; In the vestibule downstairs stand parallel and horizontal bars, while in the vestibule upstairs is a joiner's bench . . . .

90

In the village, people rise with the fires. . . . Half-an-hour after the ringing of the bell, there appear in the mist, in the rain, or in the oblique rays of the autumnal sun, dark figures, by twos, by threes, or singly. . . . The children have nothing with them – neither reading books nor copy-books. . . . They are not vexed by the thought of the impending lessons. They bring with them nothing but their impressionable natures, and their convictions that today it will be as jolly in school as it was yesterday. No one is ever rebuked for being late, and they never are late, except in the case of some of the older ones, whose fathers now and then keep them back to do some work. In such cases they come running to school at full speed, and all out of breath. So long as the teacher has not yet arrived they gather near the porch, pushing each other off the steps, or sliding on the frozen crust of the smooth road, while some go to the schoolrooms. If it is cold, they read, write or play, waiting for the teacher.

The boys . . . never addressed any one [girl] in particular, but always all collectively: 'O girls, why don't you skate?' . . . There is only one girl . . . about ten years of age, whom the boys treat as their equal except for a delicate shade of politeness and with reserve.[1]

<hr />

Tolstoy had the remarkable ability to remember his own childhood in detail, with all its sensations and experiences. It gave him an understanding of the child mind, both in his teaching and in the way he wrote about children in his books. Most of us have forgotten, have buried and sublimated, the children we once were, so that the keen intuition of childhood, if remembered at all, is distorted by adult criteria. A safety factor also operates, obliterating from our consciousness early impressions which are painful or shameful. Most of us no longer truly understand who we were as children.

Tolstoy was a rare exception. His perceptions were so acute, from his earliest years, that he retained vividly that knowledge of childhood which so many people discard. He knew himself as few people care to do. Knowledge of oneself to such an extent is neither comfortable nor easy to live with.

He knew, remembering, that a child is very much aware of its own value. He understood what can lie behind the tears of a child.

Poor Ilinka was probably crying not so much from physical pain as at the thought that five boys, whom he may have liked, had for no reason at all conspired to detest and persecute him.[2]

Tolstoy's own first tutor had been the kindly and elderly Feodor Ivanovitch, of whom he drew a loving portrait in *Childhood* as a good honest man, fond of children. As the boy in that book grows up, the old man has to go. In his place comes a new and younger tutor, whose methods are scientific and strict, and who has no wish to know the mind of a child. Self-opinionated and arrogant, he demands above all respect for his authority. Tolstoy writes of the child's distress in a darkened room after an unmerited caning by the new tutor.

> I did not cry but something heavy as stone lay on my heart. All sorts of thoughts and fancies whirled through my troubled brain but the recollection of the disasters that had befallen me continually interrupted their fantastic sequence, and I found myself in a hopeless maze of conjectures as to the fate in store for me, of despair and of dread. [3]

His delight in children is to be found in many places in his books. He never underestimated them. They're never just stock characters or merely part of the background, but persons in their own right. His understanding of a young person's emotions is never flawed by sentimentality.

> 'Remember, my little Nikolai', [said Mama,] 'that no one will love you for your face so you must try to be a sensible good boy.' . . .

> I often had moments of despair, fancying that there could be no earthly happiness for a person with such a broad nose, such thick lips and such small grey eyes as I had; and I prayed for a miracle that would transform me into a handsome man, and I would have given all I possessed and everything I might have in the future in exchange for a handsome face. [4]

> It was getting dark by the time we reached home. Mamma sat down at the piano, and we children fetched paper, pencils and paints, and settled ourselves at the round table to draw. I only had blue paint; but for all that I took it into my head to draw a picture of the hunt. After representing in very lively style a blue boy on a blue horse, and some blue dogs, I stopped, uncertain whether one could paint a blue hare, and ran into Papa's study to consult him. Papa was reading something and in answer to my question 'Are there blue hares?' replied without lifting his head 'Yes, my dear, there are.' Returning to the round table, I painted a blue hare, but then found it necessary to turn it into a bush. I did not like the bush either and made it into a tree, then the tree into a hayrick, and the hayrick into a cloud, until finally I had so smeared my whole sheet of paper with blue paint that I tore it up in vexation and went off to meditate in the high-backed arm-chair. [5]

At lunch Grisha began whistling and, what was worse, was disobedient to the English governess, and had to go without pudding. Dolly would not have let things go so far on such a day had she been present; but she was obliged to uphold the English governess, and confirmed her decision that Grisha should have no pudding. This rather spoiled the general happiness.

Grisha cried, declaring that Nikolinka had whistled too, but they did not punish him, and that he wasn't crying about the pudding – he didn't mind that – but because it wasn't fair. This was too pathetic, and Dolly decided to speak to the governess and get her to forgive Grisha, and went to find her. But as she was passing the drawing-room she beheld a scene which filled her heart with such joy that tears came into her eyes and she pardoned the little delinquent herself.

The culprit was sitting in the corner by the window; beside him stood Tanya with a plate. On the plea of wanting to give her dolls some dinner, she had obtained the governess's permission to take her pudding to the nursery, and had brought it instead to her brother. Still weeping over the unfairness of his punishment, he was eating the pudding, and kept saying through his sobs 'You have some too . . . let's eat it together . . . together.'

Tanya, affected at first by her pity for Grisha, and then by a sense of her own noble action, also had tears in her eyes; but she did not refuse, and ate her share.

When they caught sight of their mother, they were dismayed; but, looking into her face, they saw they were not doing wrong and, with their mouths full, began to laugh and wipe their smiling lips with their hands, smearing their beaming faces all over with tears and jam.[6]

—◦◇◦—

Written over the portals of his school at Yasnaya Polyana were the words 'Come and Go Freely'. He was greatly concerned that the Russia of his time (which he saw as a backward, despotic, and oligarchic society) should not adopt the authoritarian rules of education which he found in use in Germany and elsewhere. The imposition of a rigid structure of State-accredited truths seemed to him a gross invasion of the rights of the individual. An educational system should be adaptable to the needs of the Russian people, and not solely to those of their masters. Above all, he abhorred the implementation of judgments, of suspect interpretations of truth, handed down from Government officials into the malleable minds of the children.

An uncompromising individualist himself, he understood how much a child needed to be free to form its own judgments. Not that classroom freedom was to be classroom anarchy. On the contrary, it would make possible a partnership, a two-way involvement, with the man teaching the child and the child teaching the man. The more children instructed themselves, the more amenable to order they became. The more they themselves felt the need for this self-imposed order the greater became the master's influence over them.

Attempts to regiment children he saw as inevitably self-defeating. The inflexible rules laid down by the Government for its schools were only an illusion of the order they thought they were creating. He wrote of officialdom's 'strange attitude towards *imaginary* children. Not real children at all, not children that *I* have ever seen in Russia.'[7]

Teachers operating the State system did not sufficiently comprehend those they were presuming to teach. In his estimation they were not teachers at all, merely sterile administrators. A teacher had to be something more – a sympathetic psychologist capable of fathoming the child's soul. State pedagogues could not understand a child's instinctive mistrust of all that is false. They could not begin to realise what might be at the root of a stubborn inability to learn. He saw it as a child's defence against teaching which is pointless and unrelated to life.

It would be very easy to do as some writers about Tolstoy have done, and denigrate his theories as being naïve and impracticable. His ideas can be seen as ridiculously optimistic, founded on an egocentric paternalism. It long ago became the fashion to present Tolstoy as a humourless man, childish and selfish. Maybe he was at times all of these things. A great man can be as ridiculous as a small one. The vehemence of some of the outbursts in his diaries can be interpreted in translation as comically obtuse and self-dramatising. But I don't believe that the man who so often set reality down on paper, with such unflinching honesty, was as naïve as some would make out. The man attempting to lift the Russian educational system up by its bootstraps was the same man who had already written the *Sevastopol Sketches*, and who would later come to grips with moral issues in a way which was to command the respect of the world.

What he tried to create was a practical system based on a combination of common sense, kindliness, and the stimulation of latent imaginative powers. This would, he believed, eventually receive the spontaneous support of not only the children but also their parents. He could envisage a time when not the bureaucrats but the people themselves would decide where schools should be built, appoint the masters, and see their children growing in stature because of what the school brought out in them.

Tolstoy in 1868

He reproached the State for brutally interfering, for closing down schools, and substituting for large numbers of small manageable ones a smaller number of larger ones. He was advocating a better, a more truthful, and so more valuable kind of schooling than the State was inclined to provide. It was a model which the State would be at liberty to adopt. Of course, it did nothing of the kind.

⊷◇⊶

He founded an educational periodical and named it after the house and his first school – Yasnaya Polyana. It was an experiment, a forum for the discussion of how best to educate young minds, and it lasted for twelve monthly numbers. The first began with an appeal to the public:

> Entering on a new work, I am under some fear both for myself and for those thoughts which have been for years developing in me and which I regard as true. ... I shall be glad to provide room for all opinions in my magazines. Of one thing only am I afraid – ... that the discussion of a subject so dear and important to us all as that of national education may degenerate into sarcasms personalities and journalistic polemics. ... I therefore beg all future opponents of my views to express their thoughts so that ... I might agree with my opponents when the error of my view is proved.[8]
>
> Count L.N. Tolstoy

The twelve issues contained some interesting articles relating to both the theory of education and its practice. He addressed the following advice to teachers:

> Every teacher ... must, by regarding every imperfection in the pupil's comprehension not as showing a defect in the pupil but a defect in his own instruction, endeavour to develop in himself the ability of discovering new methods.[9]

He went on to define four terms; education, training, instruction, and teaching.

> *Education* is ... the sum total of all those influences which develop man, give him a broader outlook and new knowledge. ... Books, work, study, ... art, science, life – all these educate. As do playground games, and also the suffering of children from unfair punishments inflicted upon them.
>
> *Training* is the influence exercised by one man on another for the purpose of making him adopt certain moral habits.
>
> *Instruction* is the transmission of knowledge from one person to another (one can be instructed in chess, or history, or bootmaking). *Teaching*, an aspect of instruction, is the influence exercised by one man upon another for the purpose of leading him to acquire certain accomplishments (to sing, to do carpentering, to dance, to row, to recite). Instruction and teaching are means of education when they are exercised without compulsion ... and means of training when teaching is compulsory and ... when only those subjects are given which the teacher regards as necessary.[10]

He was opposed to the separate interrogation of individual children in front of the class. He reasoned that this placed a child in an abnormal situation wherein that child is unable to do himself justice and did not dare put any originality of thought into his replies. This might be from timidity, or fear, or perhaps from mistrust of his own abilities, or from shyness in front of the others. Possibly because of having been humiliated by the master on an earlier occasion. Sometimes failure to answer a question correctly might come from a confusion in the child's mind, the question having been asked just at the very moment when his curiosity had been awakened to some other aspect of the matter. At such a time it would be more valuable to obtain a question from the child rather than oblige him to answer one by rote.

There was nothing more harmful to the development of children than this system of interrogating each child in turn within a rigid superior-inferior teacher-pupil relationship. Tolstoy preferred to let children discuss their views

Tolstoy teaching in the school at Yasnaya Polyana from the painting by A. A. Plastova

freely together. He remembered having seen an elderly teacher inflicting ridicule and humiliation on a pupil, knowing the child to be suffering, seeing him blush and break out into perspiration, and yet continuing with the inquisition. 'Nothing', he wrote, angrily, 'is more revolting to me than such a sight!'[11]

He disapproved also of conventional written examinations. It might appear that a child was being taught history or mathematics but in fact he was merely being trained in the quite different accomplishment of giving the required answers to examination questions. Tolstoy did not consider this kind of training as particularly valuable as an end in itself.

—◦◇◦—

A frequent theme in his books is the parent's lack of understanding of the child:

The lesson consisted in learning by heart some verses from the Gospel, and repeating the beginning of the Old Testament. The verses from the Gospel Seriozha knew fairly well, but just as he was reciting them he became so absorbed in watching a bone in his father's forehead, which turned so abruptly at the temples, that he got mixed up and put the end of one verse on to the beginning of another where the same word occurred. Karenin concluded that he did not understand what he was saying, and this irritated him.

He frowned, and began explaining what Seriozha had heard dozens of times before and could never remember, because he understood it too well, just as he could not remember that 'suddenly' is an adverb of manner of action.

Seriozha looked at his father with scared eyes, and could think of nothing but whether his father would make him repeat what he had just said, as he sometimes did. He was so terrified at the thought that he no longer understood anything. However, his father did not make him repeat it, and passed on to the lesson from the Old Testament. Seriozha related the events themselves well enough, but when it came to answering questions as to what some of the events foretold, he knew nothing, though he had been punished before over this lesson. The passage about which he could not say anything at all, and at which he began floundering and cutting the table and rocking his chair, was where he had to repeat the patriarchs before the Flood. He did not know one of them, except Enoch, who had been taken up to heaven alive. Last time he had remembered their names, but now he could only think of Enoch, chiefly because Enoch was his favourite character in the whole of the Old Testament, and attached to Enoch's being taken up alive to heaven there was a whole train of thought to which he surrendered himself now while he stared at his father's watch-chain and a half-unfastened button on his waistcoat.

. . . 'This is bad, Seriozha, very bad. If you don't try to learn the things that are more necessary than anything for a Christian,' said his father, getting up, 'whatever can interest you? I am not pleased with you, . . . I shall have to punish you.'

His father and his teacher were both dissatisfied with Seriozha, and he certainly did learn his lessons very badly. Yet it could not be said that he was a stupid boy. On the contrary, he was far cleverer than the boys his teacher held up as examples to Seriozha. In his father's opinion, he did not try to learn what he was taught. As a matter of fact, he could not learn it. He could not, because his soul was full of other more urgent claims than those his father and the teacher made upon him. Those claims were in opposition, and he was in direct conflict with his instructors.

He was nine years old; he was a child; but he knew his own soul and treasured it, guarding it as the eyelid guards the eye, and without the key of love he let no one into his heart. His teachers complained that he would not learn, while his soul was thirsting for knowledge.[11]

—◦◇◦—

Tolstoy taught composition in what was in those days a totally unheard-of fashion, by involving himself in a friendly rivalry with his pupils. He would start by writing a few lines. The children would want to see what he had written, and were then invited to comment. They would be dissatisfied with various details, and would correct him, suggesting fresh metaphors and situations, further developments of the story and so on. Composition became, in this way, a collective enterprise, and he encouraged and greatly valued the originality of their thought.

He had a fresh approach also to the teaching of History. His personal experience suggested to him that the first spark of interest in History as a subject came when the pupils began to have an understanding of contemporary events, and when they began to see that they themselves were by their actions part of the making of History.

His pupils' liking for school may well have been due in part to his skill as a story-teller. Everything suggests that he was as much a spell-binder with the spoken as with the written word. No doubt the village children listened to him as attentively as literate adults read his books. The subjects on which he drew included his adventures as a young soldier in the Caucasus – though with certain omissions, one hopes! There were stories about his encounters with bears, the character and sagacity of his favourite dogs, and he retold in his own way tales from the Arabian Nights.

He wrote a number of folk tales and fairy stories, making no secret of the fact that the schoolchildren had a share in the writing of them. Such co-operation seemed to him admirable, and he was always very proud of it. One of the tales written by this method was *The Peasant and the Cucumbers*.

> A peasant once went to a vegetable garden to steal cucumbers.
> 'I'll carry off this sack of cucumbers,' he thought, 'and with the money I get for them I'll buy a hen. The hen will lay eggs, she will sit on them and hatch a brood of chicks, and I'll feed the chicks till they grow, then I'll sell them and buy a suckling pig. I'll feed the suckling pig till it grows into a sow, I'll breed her, she'll have a litter of pigs, and I'll sell them. With the money I get for the pigs I'll buy a mare. She will foal, I'll feed the foals till they grow, then I'll sell them. With the money I get for the foals I'll buy a house with a garden. I'll plant cucumbers in the garden, and I won't let anyone steal them

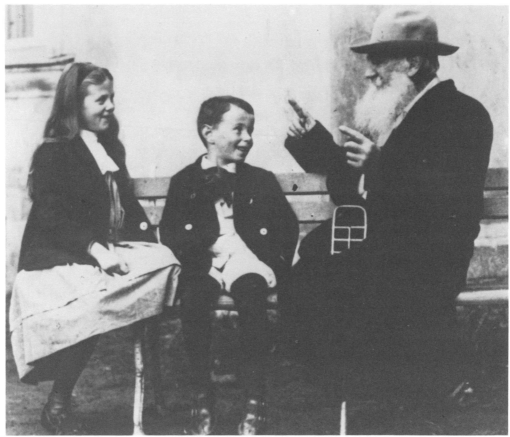

Tolstoy, as an old man, telling his grandchildren the story of the cucumbers.

   – I'll keep guard over them. I'll hire a strong watchman, and from time to time I'll go out to the garden and shout: ''Hey, you! Take care!'' '

   The peasant was so carried away by his thoughts that he completely forgot he was in someone else's garden, and he shouted at the top of his voice.

   The watchman heard him and came running out. He caught the peasant and gave him a good beating.[12]

Sometimes he would race the children out of the schoolroom to the woods, like an older boy with young brothers. His own enquiring mind prompted them to ask questions about everything they saw or heard. They would fish together in the pond, and in the winter would skate and make snowmen, and he would throw snowballs with the best of them.

From the very beginning he determined that in any school under his supervision there should be no high desk for the master. A teacher should not hold forth from a rostrum, as from a pulpit. He should operate instead from among the children, never from a position which suggested privilege and authority.

His methods were deplored by the authorities in Moscow. 'Come and Go freely' indeed! How could the education of the children of the masses be carried on if the pupils were at liberty to come and go as they wished? How could the children be permitted to decide among themselves how much they should learn? Pupils from schools such as this could not be trained to become useful obedient subjects of an autocratic government. To such criticisms he replied that it was not the business of schools to train but to educate, which was something quite different.

He passed no moral judgments. Instead, as always, he put his opponents' point of view for them, with such devastating clarity that it stood condemned by its own specious logic. It was reasonable that the State wished to train, for it needed men for various purposes, to fit into niches already prepared for them. The Church also wanted children to be trained, so that they would obey, and believe without thought everything they were told. He really was a maddening person for officialdom to come up against. What a pity, they felt, that he had so many important relatives in high places ...

The future author of *War and Peace* was not a man to be blind to the lessons of history. He held that the peasant could live without Society, but Society could not live without the peasant. This was an explosive thought to put into the minds of the peasant millions. Small wonder that the authorities, studying his pronouncements, saw him as a growing threat.

A friend of his, E. Markof, gave an eye-witness account of what happened next.

> Tolstoy warmly sympathised with the liberation of the serfs and naturally acted in a direction which provoked a large majority of landowners against him. He has received a number of threatening letters; they threatened to knock him down or shoot him in a duel and he has been denounced to the authorities. It so happened that at the very time when the magazine *Yasnaya Polyana* was started by Tolstoy, proclamations of different revolutionary parties made their appearance in St. Petersburg and the police were actively engaged searching for the hidden printing press ....

> In the absence of Tolstoy his house was being kept by his elderly aunt and his sister was staying there with her children on a visit. Our common friend

G.A. Auerbach and myself were spending the summer with our families at a distance of about five versts. ... Early one morning, a messenger from Yasnaya Polyana arrived. We were requested to come as soon as possible on important business. Auerbach and I jumped into a waggonette and hurried on as hard as we could. On our entering the courtyard we were faced with a real invasion .... The head of the police district, the commissar of rural police, local police, witnesses, and in addition to all this – gendarmes. The colonel of the gendarmes arrived with jingling and bustle, ... to the great consternation of the village people. After some difficulty we succeeded in entering the house. The poor ladies were almost fainting .... Everything was opened, thrown about, turned upside down – tables, drawers, wardrobes, chests of drawers, boxes, caskets, etc. Crowbars were used in the stables to lift the floors; the ponds in the park were searched by means of nets in order to catch the criminal printing press, instead of which only innocent carp and crabs made their appearance.

It need hardly be said that in the first place the unfortunate school had been turned upside down; but finding nothing there the searchers went in the same noisy, bustling procession, with sounding bells to pay a visit apparently to all the seventeen schools of the district, everywhere turning over tables, ... carrying off exercise books and school manuals, putting the teachers under arrest.[13]

Zakharyin Yakunin in his *Reminiscences of the Countess A.A. Tolstoy* gives some further details:

A great shock ... [was] suffered by his aunt and his sister ... The police commissioner ... gave permission to Tolstoy's sister to leave the study after he had read before her, and in the presence of two gendarmes, all those intimate letters ... as well as Tolstoy's diary, and everything Tolstoy had written and kept hidden from all since the age of sixteen.[14]

Prince Oblonsky wrote of the same incident in his *Reminiscences*:

The school at Yasnaya Polyana was getting on splendidly. But ... the authorities did not very much favour it and suspected that there must be something politically unsound in Yasnaya Polyana.[15]

Tolstoy was away at Samarra, taking the kumiss cure (the drinking of large quantities of fermented mare's milk) for his chronic indigestion but, on hearing of the violation of his house and the schools, cut short his medical treatment and returned to Yasnaya Polyana.

What a very lucky thing it is that I was not at home! If I had been, I should by this time have had to be tried for murder! ... This affair I do not wish to and positively *cannot* leave alone. All the employment in which I had found happiness and peace is spoilt ... As to the landowners, there is, it goes without saying, one outburst of delight. I have no other choice than ... to receive satisfaction as public as the insult.[16]

Learning from his aunt, the Countess A.A. Tolstoy, that on leaving the Colonel of the Gendarmes had threatened her with further searches until he succeeded in finding what was hidden, Tolstoy observed grimly, 'Loaded pistols are in my room, and I am waiting to see how all this will end!' He made an emphatic complaint directly to the Tsar, Alexander II, personally handing him in Moscow a written account of the outrage.

There ensued an interesting correspondence between two Government Departments.

The Minister of the Interior to the Minister of Instruction:

3.10.1862

The careful reading of the educational review *Yasnaya Polyana*, edited by Count Tolstoy, leads to the conclusion that this review, in preaching new methods of tuition ... frequently spreads ideas ... which are injurious ... I consider it necessary to draw the attention of your Excellency to the general tendency and spirit of the review, which very often attacks the fundamental rules of religion and morality. The continuation of the review in the same spirit must, in my opinion, be considered the more dangerous as its editor is a man of a remarkable and one may say even a fascinating talent, who cannot be suspected to be a criminal or an unprincipled man. The evil lies in the sophistry and eccentricity of his convictions which, being expounded with extraordinary eloquence, may carry away inexperienced teachers in this direction, and thus give a wrong turn to popular education. I have the honour to inform you of this hoping you may consider it useful to draw the special attention of the censor to this publication.[17]

On receipt of this request, the Minister of Public Instruction issued an order for the examination of the printed numbers of the review *Yasnaya Polyana*. On October 24th, he informed the Minister of the Interior that in accordance with the examination and the report upon it presented to him by his subordinates, he saw nothing dangerous or contrary to religion in the review.

On the whole, I must say that Count Tolstoy's work as an educationist deserves full respect, and the Ministry of Public Instruction is bound to help him and give him encouragement, even though not sharing all his views, which, after maturer consideration, he will probably give up himself.[18]

The Minister of Public Instruction was mistaken. Tolstoy did not give up his ideas. He ceased to publish *Yasnaya Polyana*, but it may well have been the very violence of the bigoted attack upon him which led him eventually to move on to propagate his beliefs on a wider stage. His answer to the ransacking of the schools and the brutal invasion of his house would one day be his thunderous denunciation of those in authority.

Later that year he gave up his personal supervision of the schools, putting aside, for the time being, his experiment in education. He had another even more engrossing experiment to preoccupy him. He had decided to marry Sonya, one of the three attractive daughters of his physician, Dr. Behrs.

His finances were sadly in need of replenishment, never having recovered from his heavy gambling losses, and it was in the hope of improving this situation that he now settled down to write in earnest. First he finished off *The Cossacks*, one of the most exuberant and enjoyable of his books, which he had begun ten years earlier in the Caucasus. And then he embarked upon what has often been described as the greatest novel ever written, *War and Peace*. The task he undertook was immense. Yet the detail is so exact, the many strands of that vast book so interwoven but distinct. No film or television version has ever been able to do justice to it, not even the eight hour Russian epic. They are all, inevitably, potted versions alongside the tremendous power and sweep of the book itself.

In the period of several years which elapsed between the completion of *War and Peace* and the commencement of *Anna Karenina* he again opened a school at Yasnaya Polyana; this time more discreetly within the house itself instead of in a separate building. There were thirty-five pupils, children of the local peasants. The old obsession flared once more, paternalistic and fulfilling, the pupils becoming an extension of his own family. It was very much a family affair now, the other members of the teaching staff being Sonya, his eight-year-old son Sergei, and his daughter Tanya, who was seven.

He had at this time, and for some years to come, a very good relationship with his own children. He played energetic games with them, and told them bedtime stories as from the mind of a child. He would gallop up and down the staircase with delighted and shrieking children perched on his shoulders and clinging round his neck, in a boisterous activity known in the family as the Charge of the Numidian Cavalry. Afterwards, to calm them down in readiness for bed, he would tell them to stand in the corner, face the floral wallpaper, and try very hard *not* to think about a White Bear. . . .

There was a good deal of happy laughter at Yasnaya Polyana in those days. He made a wooden letter-box, and hung it on the wall of the landing. Into the box they were all of them encouraged to post verses of their own composition, original stories, jokes, riddles, comments about other members of the family. Each Sunday all would be summoned to a ceremonial opening of the box, and its contents would be read aloud. He put into the box what he called the Case Book of the Yasnaya Polyana Asylum:

> Case No. 1. L.N. Tolstoy. One of the harmless sort. The patient is subject to the mania known to doctors as 'World Reform Delusion'. His hallucination consists in thinking that you can change other people's lives by words. General symptoms: Busying himself with unsuitable occupations such as cleaning and making boots, mowing hay, and so forth.

> Case No. 2. Countess S.A. Tolstoy. Belongs also to the harmless sort, but sometimes has to be suppressed. The patient is subject to the 'Hurry Scurry Mania'. Her hallucination consists of thinking that everyone demands so much of her and that she cannot manage to get everything done. Symptoms: Straining to solve problems which don't exist; answering questions before they've been put; refuting accusations which have never been brought; satisfying demands that haven't been made. Treatment: Hard work, diet, and avoidance of frivolous worldly people.[19]

He engaged a pretty young English girl, Hannah Tracey, to be the children's nurse. Careful and efficient, she insisted on absolute cleanliness, always bathing her charges in completely cold water. Over the years she was to become very much a member of the family, looked upon by the girls especially not as a paid employee but as a much-loved aunt. The children were forbidden by their father ever to give Hannah or any of the other servants an order, but always to ask very politely for anything they wanted.

Incensed by continuing bureaucratic interference, he seriously contemplated uprooting himself from Russia and living permanently in England with his wife and children. He planned to buy a house in London and a farm near the coast, perhaps on the Sussex Downs, behind Brighton. It's an intriguing picture; had he followed up this sudden enthusiasm would the Tolstoys have joined the ranks of those illustrious immigrés from Central Europe who did so much to invigorate the intellectual life of Britain during Victoria's reign? He even went so far as to canvass friends for letters of introduction to important people in English society, but then he received a conciliatory letter from the officials who had offended him, and he dropped the idea.

As young children his sons and daughters all adored him and had no doubt that he was the best of fathers. But not all those who rode on his shoulders in

Tolstoy among the children of the peasants of Yasnaya Polyana in 1909

that domestic cavalry charge would live long enough to take a more searching look in his direction. Sonya had in all thirteen children by him. Three were to die while he was writing *Anna Karenina*, and two others would journey only to an early grave, victims of the child-killing illnesses of the time. He had promised *Anna Karenina* in instalments to *The Russian Herald*, which meant he had to meet a series of deadlines. It was the treadmill known to many writers in those days. Continuing to teach while writing these regular chapters, he came to resent the demands his fictional characters made upon him. His work in the schoolroom was a lifeline. 'I simply cannot tear myself away from living beings to bother about imaginary ones. Art is a beautiful lie. I can lie no longer.'[20]

He was drawing close to a great crisis in his life. Moral questions were tearing him apart, giving him no rest. It seemed to him quite simply wrong that he should own land, property, even the copyright of his own books, while the peasants were suffering poverty and ignorance in their millions. He became very depressed following the death of his small son Nikolai, after many days and nights of agony from fluid on the brain, and was haunted by memories of the death of his brother of the same name. A few months later Sonya gave birth to a daughter who lived for only half an hour. At a desperately low ebb, he formed a plan to establish now not a school but a teacher training college in the house, and went to the length of equipping rooms with desks and benches for the purpose. When, to his bitter disappointment, there were almost no applicants to be trained by him, he abandoned the project in despair.

106

Tolstoy and his family at Yasnaya Polyana in 1887.

Always a harsh critic of his own writing, he had no faith in *Anna Karenina* and was utterly taken aback by its success. Engrossed to the exclusion of all else with what to him were the crucial issues facing mankind, he had taken to working in a virtually soundproof ground floor room with a vaulted ceiling. It was sparsely furnished with a writing table, a few shabby chairs covered in black oilskin, and the hard narrow couch on which he and all his children had been born. On the wall hung the portrait of Charles Dickens, flanked by another of Schopenhauer. Here he composed pamphlets and articles on religious and ethical themes, which, even more than his novels, were to cause eminent men to write to him from all over the world.

It was a time of a hardening of attitudes at Yasnaya Polyana. Sonya had no sympathy with his cosmic concern for the suffering millions outside the family, and his second son Ilya would one day write about the changes that came in the late seventies:

> It was my father, of course, who suffered most. He became taciturn, morose, and irritable, and our former jovial bouyant companion and leader was transformed before our eyes into a stern and censorious preacher. . . . We felt a severe split in our lives, felt that something important was missing as *papa* grew more and more remote from us.[21]

More than thirty years of life still lay ahead of him. Biographers have documented his championing of the persecuted Dukhobors, his herculean efforts to aid the victims of the years of famine, his excommunication, his condemnation of the Russo-Japanese war, his correspondence with Shaw, Gandhi and others. The story has often been told of the increasing stresses within his marriage, his flight from Yasnaya Polyana, and his death at the railway station of Astapovo. All these things are of great interest but are outside the scope of this book.

———◇◇◇◇———

It is perhaps a reflection of the importance that education and the contact with children had on him that near the end of his life Tolstoy wrote to his Russian biographer, Paul Biryukov:

> I owe the brightest time of my life not to the love of woman, but to love of people, to the love of children. That was a wonderful time . . .[22]

Tolstoy with his granddaughter, Tanya in 1909

Notes

Early Life

1 From 'Sevastopol in December', in **Tales of Sevastopol,** Foreign Languages Publishing House, Moscow (1946).
2 Tolstoy's diary entry for 11 April 1855, quoted by Troyat, p.120.
3 Tolstoy's diary entry for 2–5 March 1855, quoted in Maude, **The Private Diary of Leo Tolstoy.**
4 Quoted in Maude, **Life of Tolstoy,** p.129.
5 Letter from Turgenev to Druzhinin, written in 1856, quoted by Ilya Tolstoy in his reminiscences.
6 From one of Tolstoy's educational articles published in *Yasnaya Polyana,* quoted by Biryukov, p. 316 ff.
7 Quoted by Biryukov, p. 274.
8 Quoted by Biryukov, p. 275.
9 Tolstoy's diary entry for 13 October 1860, quoted by Troyat, p. 200.
10 From Tolstoy's article 'On Popular Education' published in **Yasnaya Polyana,** quoted in Biryukov, p. 287 ff.

Nineteenth-Century England

1 Report of the Royal Commission on Housing, 1880s.
2 Charles Dickens, **Dombey and Son,** The Clarendon Dickens, edited by Alan Horsman, Oxford University Press (1974), p. 462.
3 Nikolaus Pevsner, **The Buildings of England (London),** Penguin (1952), p. 35.

Tolstoy's Visit

1 Quoted by Troyat, p. 203.
2 Quoted by Maude in **Family Views of Tolstoy,** p. 71.
3 Ibid.
4 Ibid.
5 Fyodor Dostoievsky, **Summer Impressions,** translated by Kyril FitzLyon, John Calder (1955).

Education in England

1 Quoted by David Craig in his introduction to Charles Dickens, **Hard Times,** Penguin (1969).
2 Quoted in the entry on Joseph Lancaster in the **Dictionary of National Biography.**
3 Charles Dickens, **Hard Times,** Oxford Illustrated Dickens, Oxford University Press (1955).
4 **Epitome of some of the chief events and transactions in the life of Joseph Lancaster,** New Haven, Connecticut, 1833.
5 Quoted in the entry on Andrew Bell in the **Dictionary of National Biography.**

12 March 1861

1 Tolstoy Museum, Moscow.
2 Covent Garden Market was so described in an article in **Punch** of 14 August 1880, entitled 'Covent Garden: Mud-Salad Market' though this may not be the first use of the phrase.
3 **Cassell's Book of Sports and Pastimes,** Cassell, Petter, Galpin & Co., (1881).
4 Ibid.
5 Ibid.
6 H. S. Simmonds, **All About Battersea,** London (1882).
7 From an article 'Tolstoy in Weimar', by Dr Von Bode, published in **Der Saemann,** quoted by Biryukov, p. 292 ff.
8 Quoted by Biryukov, p. 295.

Return to Russia

1 From Tolstoy's article 'The School at Yasnaya Polyana' published in **Yasnaya Polyana,** quoted by Biryukov, p. 319.
2 From 'Childhood', Chapter 19, in **Childhood, Boyhood, Youth,** translated by Rosemary Edmonds, Penguin (1964).
3 Ibid. 'Boyhood', Chapter 15.
4 Ibid. 'Childhood', Chapter 11.
5 Ibid. 'Childhood', Chapter 17.
6 **Anna Karenin,** translated by Rosemary Edmonds, Penguin (1954), p. 285.
7 Quoted by Baudouin, **Tolstoi: the Teacher.**
8 Quoted by Biryukov, p. 324.

9   From 'On methods of teaching to read and write', published in
    Yasnaya Polyana, quoted by Biryukov, p. 326.
10 From 'Education and Instruction', published in **Yasnaya Polyana,**
    quoted by Biryukov, p. 327.
11 **Anna Karenin,** translated by Rosemary Edmonds, Penguin (1954),
    p. 553.
12 From Tolstoy's **First Reader** (1872), in **Fables and Fairy Tales** by Leo
    Tolstoy, translated by Ann Dunnigan, New American Library (1962).
13 From an article printed in the **Messenger of Europe,** quoted by
    Biryukov, p. 349.
14 Quoted by Biryukov, p. 351.
15 Ibid.
16 Ibid, p. 352.
17 Ibid.
18 Ibid, p. 353.
19 Quoted by Lady Cynthia Asquith in **Married to Tolstoy.**
20 Quoted by Troyat, p. 348.
21 Ilya Tolstoy, **Tolstoy, My Father,** pp. 169–70.
22 Quoted by Troyat.

Bibliography

Lady Cynthia Asquith, **Married to Tolstoy,** Hutchinson (1960)
Louis Charles Baudouin, **Tolstoi: the Teacher,** translated by Fred Rothwell, Kegan Paul & Co. (1923)
Paul Biryukov, **Leo Tolstoy: His Life and Work,** Heinemann (1906)
Edward Crankshaw, **Tolstoy: The Making of a Novelist,** Weidenfeld & Nicolson (1974).
E. H. Crosby, **Tolstoy as a Schoolmaster,** London (1904)
Aylmer Maude, **The Life of Tolstoy** (2 Vols.), Oxford University Press (1930)
Aylmer Maude (ed.), **Family Views of Tolstoy,** translated by Louise and Aylmer Maude, George Allen & Unwin (1926)
——, **The Private Diary of Leo Tolstoy 1853–1857,** translated by Louise and Aylmer Maude, Heinemann (1927)
R. J. Mitchell and M. D. R. Leys, **A History of London Life,** Longmans Green & Co. (1958)
Iona and Peter Opie, **Children's Games in Street and Playground,** Oxford University Press (1969)
E. J. Simmons, **Leo Tolstoy,** Little, Brown, New York (1946)
Edward A. Steiner, **Tolstoy, the Man and his Message,** Fleming H. Revell Co., New York (1909)
Countess Alexandra Tolstoy, **A Life of My Father,** translated by Elizabeth Reynolds Hapgood, Harper & Bros, New York (1953)
Count Ilya Tolstoy, **Tolstoy, My Father,** translated by Ann Dunnigan, Peter Owen Ltd (1972)
Henri Troyat, **Tolstoy,** translated from the French by Nancy Amphoux, Doubleday & Co. Inc., New York (1967)